DIGITAL TWIN TECHNOLOGIES IN BUSINESS

Building Smarter, Safer, Faster Operations

Reduce Risk, Cut Costs, and Transform Your
Enterprise with Real-Time Virtual Models

Irvin K. Appell

Disclaimer:

The advice and strategies contained herein may only be suitable for some situations. This work is sold with the understanding that the author and publisher are not engaged in rendering professional services. If professional assistance is required, the services of a competent professional should be sought. The author and publisher specifically disclaim any liability incurred from the use or application of the contents of this book.

Table of Contents

Introduction

The Mirror That Knows the Future

What if your business had a second brain—one that could watch, think, learn, and act before anything ever went wrong?

What if your factory could simulate every production run before a single machine powered up?
What if your city could see a traffic jam before it formed—and prevent it altogether?
What if a digital replica of your heart could warn your doctor of a problem you couldn't feel yet?

This isn't science fiction. It's already happening.

In Shanghai, a living, breathing digital version of the city maps traffic, monitors energy, and adjusts public services in real time. In Barcelona, researchers are creating virtual models of human hearts—down to the cellular level—to predict heart disease before symptoms ever appear. Inside Intel and other pioneering organizations, invisible engines track every moving part of a machine, detect potential failures before they happen, and optimize operations minute by minute, across entire networks.

These are not futuristic dreams—they're digital twins. And they're going to either save your business—or replace it.

Across industries, the rules have changed. Reacting isn't enough. Planning isn't fast enough. Businesses now face pressure from every direction—consumers demanding speed, governments demanding sustainability, and competition that's already using AI to move faster than you can.

In this new reality, a digital twin is more than just a 3D model or a sensor network. It's a live, thinking mirror of your operations, one that watches your world, learns from it, and helps you act with precision. Done right, it becomes your secret weapon—a force multiplier that helps you reduce risk, cut costs, and transform your business from the inside out.

But done wrong? It's a missed opportunity. A buzzword on a slide. A half-built system no one uses.

This book is here to help you understand the difference—and to show you how to harness this powerful technology before your competitors beat you to it.

You're about to discover:
- Why digital twins are the missing link between raw data and smart decisions
- How they're already changing manufacturing, healthcare, logistics, and urban life
- What your business needs to start building its own smarter, safer, faster operation
- And how the blending of real and virtual worlds is quietly becoming the foundation of modern business

This is more than innovation.
It's survival.
It's intelligence in motion.
It's your next competitive edge.

So let's begin.

Let's look in the mirror—and see what's possible.

PART I

UNDERSTANDING THE DIGITAL TWIN REVOLUTION

Chapter 1

What Is a Digital Twin–Really?

Most people hear the term "digital twin" and picture a slick 3D model spinning on a screen. It looks cool. Maybe it even moves. But they stop there, assuming it's just another fancy visualization tool—nice to have, but not critical. The truth is, that image barely scratches the surface. A real digital twin doesn't just look like the thing it represents—it thinks, reacts, and learns from the real world it mirrors. It's not just a model; it's a living stream of insight, one that connects the physical and digital worlds in a way that's changing how businesses operate at every level.

You may already be interacting with digital twins without even realizing it. Every time your GPS reroutes you around traffic, when your smart home adjusts the thermostat before you say a word, or when a factory predicts machine failure before it happens—those are glimpses of a deeper reality. Behind the scenes, a digital version of the world is constantly learning, adapting, and guiding decisions in real time. It's easy to miss because when it works well, it feels invisible. But in today's world, that invisibility is power.

Definition Of Digital Twin

A digital twin isn't just a polished graphic spinning on a screen or a simulation tucked away in a design file. It's something far more dynamic and alive. At its core, a digital twin is a virtual version of a real-world object, system, or process—but what makes it powerful isn't the way it looks. It's the way it thinks.

Imagine a bridge that can feel the strain of heavy traffic and send alerts before a crack forms. A machine that knows when it's wearing out long before it stops working. Or a building that adjusts its energy usage in real time based on who's inside and what they're doing. That's the power of a digital twin—not just reflecting reality, but being connected to it.

This connection is what sets digital twins apart from traditional models. They're constantly fed by real-time data from sensors, cameras, control systems, and even external sources like weather feeds or GPS networks. That data doesn't just sit there—it's processed, interpreted, and used to simulate how the real thing is performing, how it might behave in the future, and what actions can be taken to improve outcomes.

In that way, a digital twin becomes more than a replica. It's a living, breathing extension of the physical world, capable of understanding context, reacting to changes, and offering insight that would otherwise be invisible. It's the difference between looking at a photograph of a car and riding in one that tells you it needs a tune-up before it breaks down.

This is what makes digital twins such a game changer for business. They aren't just digital versions of things—they're decision-making tools, risk predictors, efficiency enablers. They shift the entire relationship between the physical and digital world from reactive to proactive. And once that shift happens, you stop waiting for problems to arise—you start staying ahead of them.

Origins and Evolution of the Concept

The idea of a digital twin didn't arrive overnight—it's been quietly evolving over decades, shaped by necessity, innovation, and the constant push to bridge the gap between the physical and digital worlds.

Its roots can be traced back to early simulation and modeling efforts in aerospace and manufacturing. In the 1960s and '70s, NASA was already working with rudimentary digital replicas of spacecraft. When engineers prepared for space missions, they created detailed simulators on Earth that mirrored the real equipment in orbit. These simulators weren't just static—they were connected to data coming from the spacecraft, allowing engineers to troubleshoot issues from thousands of miles away. It wasn't called a digital twin at the time, but the essence was there: a virtual version of something physical, continuously updated with real-time information to support decision-making.

Fast forward to the early 2000s, and the term "digital twin" began to take formal shape. As computing power grew and sensor technologies advanced, the vision of a real-time, living digital counterpart to a physical object became more realistic—and more necessary. In 2002, Dr. Michael Grieves introduced the concept during a presentation on product lifecycle management at the University of Michigan. He described a system where a digital model could mirror the lifecycle of a product—from design and manufacturing to usage and eventual retirement.

What began as a product-centric vision has since expanded dramatically. With the explosion of the Internet of Things (IoT), AI, and edge computing, digital twins are no longer confined to engineering labs or high-end manufacturing floors. They're now being used to manage entire factories, simulate urban infrastructure, monitor supply chains, personalize healthcare, and optimize everything from energy grids to autonomous vehicles.

Today, we're seeing digital twins evolve into complex, connected ecosystems. They're not just digital reflections of machines—they're models of entire environments and systems. And thanks to machine learning, they're becoming increasingly intelligent, capable of not only simulating what's happening now, but forecasting what will happen next.

This shift—from passive model to predictive intelligence—is what makes the modern digital twin so powerful. What started as a tool for understanding physical systems has become a strategic technology for transforming them.

Differences Between Static Models, Simulations, and Digital Twins

At first glance, a static model, a simulation, and a digital twin might seem interchangeable. They all represent physical things in a digital format. But the differences between them are not just technical—they're fundamental. Understanding those differences is key to grasping why digital twins are such a leap forward, and why they deliver value in ways traditional tools never could.

A static model is exactly what it sounds like—a fixed, unchanging representation. Think of a 3D rendering of a product in design software. It looks like the real thing, but it doesn't move, learn, or respond. It's useful for visualization, maybe for marketing or early-stage design, but once it's created, it stays the same. It has no connection to real-world conditions or behavior.

A simulation takes it a step further. It allows you to input certain variables and see how the system might react. Engineers use simulations to test how a machine might perform under stress, how fluid flows through a pipe, or how a building reacts to wind. These are valuable tools, especially in the design and testing phase. But simulations are typically run in isolated scenarios, with pre-set assumptions. Once the simulation ends, so does the insight. There's no real-time feedback loop.

Now enter the digital twin—a living model that doesn't just simulate once, but continuously. It's connected to real-world sensors, systems, and environments. It evolves as the physical object or system it represents changes. If a machine starts vibrating more than usual, the digital twin sees it. If temperature rises in a specific area of a warehouse, the twin registers that change and may suggest adjustments or flag a risk.

Where a simulation gives you a snapshot, a digital twin offers a live stream. Where a static model is frozen in time, a digital twin is always moving forward. It doesn't just react—it can also predict, learn, and optimize, especially when combined with AI and machine learning.

That's the defining difference: a digital twin is not just a model of what something looks like—it's a model of what it is, what it's doing, and what it's about to do. It creates a bridge between the physical and digital worlds that doesn't just inform—it empowers. And in today's fast-paced, high-stakes environment, that distinction matters more than ever.

Types of Digital Twins

Digital twins come in many forms, and their impact depends heavily on what they represent. Some mirror individual machines, while others capture the flow of entire operations. Some track human health at the cellular level; others help manage entire cities. But whether small or vast, each type serves the same purpose: to reflect a real-world counterpart in a way that makes it visible, understandable, and improvable in real time.

Product twins are perhaps the most well-known. These are digital replicas of individual physical objects—engines, motors, pumps, surgical tools, or any component that has form and function. In manufacturing, a product twin can monitor the wear and tear on a piece of machinery and alert operators before failure occurs. It can test different operating conditions virtually to predict outcomes without ever risking damage to the actual equipment. These twins are especially valuable during both the design phase and in ongoing operations, where maintenance, performance, and longevity are critical.

Process twins move beyond individual parts to model workflows or sequences of operations. Imagine the steps involved in assembling a car or bottling a product on a production line. A process twin doesn't just replicate one machine—it represents how multiple components interact over time. These twins help identify inefficiencies, bottlenecks, or points of failure in complex chains. They're essential for improving throughput, safety, and quality control across entire processes.

System twins scale even further. They bring together multiple processes, machines, and components into a unified, high-level view. A system twin might represent an entire factory, a power grid, or even a global supply chain. At this level, the focus shifts to how all the moving parts work together. These twins offer strategic insight—allowing companies to test changes across interconnected operations, balance resources, reduce energy usage, or respond to disruptions before they escalate.

Human twins are emerging as some of the most groundbreaking. These digital models are built to reflect the state of individual people—tracking health indicators, biometric data, and even cellular activity. Hospitals and research institutions are already creating digital hearts and organs to better understand disease, personalize treatment, and simulate surgical procedures. The potential to predict health outcomes, test drugs virtually, and deliver precision medicine represents a seismic shift in how we approach care and prevention.

City twins take digital mirroring to the urban scale. Cities like Shanghai are already using digital twins to simulate everything from traffic flow and public transportation to waste management and emergency response. These twins help city planners test new ideas, predict outcomes, and make smarter decisions without risking real-world consequences. They provide a digital command center for urban life—blending infrastructure, data, and human behavior into one coordinated system.

Each type of digital twin serves a different purpose, but the underlying idea is the same: when we can see and understand things as they truly are—and as they could be—we make better decisions, faster. Whether it's a single machine or a city of millions, a digital twin gives us the clarity we need to operate smarter, safer, and more efficiently.

Real-World Analogy: Ring Cameras vs. Computer Spatial Awareness

To understand what makes a digital twin so different—and so powerful—it helps to compare it to something familiar. Picture a home security system with multiple Ring cameras. Each one captures video from a specific angle: front door, backyard, garage, maybe the side gate. If you're watching the feed, you can piece together what's happening. You see someone walk past the front camera, then a moment later, they appear in the backyard. You know the layout of your home, so you intuitively understand the movement. You can fill in the blanks because your brain already has a mental map of the space.

But the system itself doesn't know that. The cameras don't talk to each other. The footage is siloed. If someone appears on one feed, the system has no idea where that person came from, where they're going next, or how that movement relates to anything else. It's just a collection of isolated viewpoints.

Now imagine if the system could do what your brain does automatically. Imagine if the cameras weren't just feeding video, but were spatially aware. They knew exactly where they were placed on the property, how they were angled, and how their views overlapped. Imagine if the system could track a person moving through different zones, stitch together their movement in 3D space, and anticipate their next step—without you having to watch anything.

That's the difference Intel is working on with its digital twin technology. It's not just about recognizing objects through cameras. It's about placing that recognition within a meaningful physical context. Knowing what is seen is only part of the picture. A real digital twin understands where it is, when it happened, and how it relates to everything else.

In a factory, this kind of spatial awareness can be the difference between a safe environment and an accident waiting to happen. If a robot is about to round a blind corner and a person is walking the same path, separate systems might not catch the risk in time. But a digital twin—one that integrates all sensors and systems into a unified spatial model—can detect the potential collision before it happens and trigger a slowdown or stop.

Just like your brain maps out your home, a digital twin maps out the world around it. It connects cameras, sensors, and data streams into one intelligent perspective. And in doing so, it shifts from passive observation to active understanding. From isolated data to unified insight. That's the leap—from Ring cameras to a system that thinks like you do, but faster.

Why Businesses Should Care: Risk, Cost, Speed, Insight

For all the technical depth behind digital twins, the real reason businesses need to pay attention comes down to something far more practical: survival. In a world where margins are tight, competition is fierce, and disruptions can hit overnight, having a clearer, faster, more accurate understanding of your operations isn't just nice to have—it's a strategic necessity.

First, there's risk. Equipment fails. Systems break. People make mistakes. In high-stakes environments like manufacturing, logistics, or healthcare, even small errors can snowball into major losses—or worse, safety incidents. Digital twins help businesses see the warning signs early. They make it possible to detect a failing part before it breaks, to predict a traffic jam before it happens, or to flag a supply chain bottleneck before it causes delays. The ability to simulate and test in a virtual environment means you can uncover vulnerabilities and fix them—without putting people, products, or profits at risk.

Then there's cost. Physical prototypes, trial-and-error testing, unplanned downtime—these all come with a price. A digital twin reduces the need for expensive guesswork. You can test multiple scenarios without touching a single physical asset. You can optimize energy usage in real time, reduce waste, and avoid costly interruptions by anticipating them before they hit. Mevea's use of digital twins in product design, for example, helps companies catch issues early and build fewer prototypes—saving time and money while improving quality.

Speed is another critical factor. In fast-moving industries, the ability to respond quickly is everything. Digital twins give you real-time visibility into what's happening across your operations. They don't just show you what went wrong—they show you what's happening now, and what might happen next. That insight shortens reaction times and empowers faster decision-making. Whether it's rerouting a delivery, adjusting a production schedule, or preparing for a weather event, businesses that move faster tend to win.

And finally, there's insight—the kind that's only possible when data stops living in silos and starts working together. A true digital twin isn't just a fancy visual or a one-off simulation. It's a coordinated, constantly evolving view of your business that helps you understand not just how things are working, but why. It connects the dots between people, machines, systems, and outcomes. It gives you the clarity to make smarter choices and the confidence to innovate with less risk.

At its core, a digital twin is a decision tool. It gives you the knowledge, foresight, and agility to stay ahead. And in today's business landscape, that's not just a competitive edge—it's the difference between leading and lagging, thriving and surviving.

Understanding what a digital twin truly is means letting go of the idea that it's just a model or dashboard. It's not a passive reflection—it's an active force, fed by real-time data, grounded in physical reality, and capable of shaping outcomes before they unfold. The businesses that grasp this shift early won't just improve what they already do—they'll redefine what's possible. Because the moment you stop thinking of your operations as static and start treating them as dynamic, intelligent, and mirrored in real time... that's when you stop reacting—and start anticipating. And in a world moving this fast, that difference is everything.

Chapter 2

Why Now? The Business Case for Digital Twins

There's a moment happening right now—quiet but seismic—where the physical and digital worlds are finally syncing in real time. It's not hype anymore. It's not locked inside tech labs or limited to futuristic prototypes. Digital twins have crossed the threshold into real business, solving real problems. And the timing isn't accidental. We're living in a decade shaped by volatility: supply chains unravel overnight, customer expectations shift in real time, and sustainability is no longer optional—it's expected. Businesses can't afford to guess anymore. They need clarity, adaptability, and speed. Digital twins offer all three.

This isn't about chasing shiny new tools. It's about responding to the pressures that are already here—and outpacing the ones still coming. Because what used to be a competitive advantage is quickly becoming the minimum standard for survival.

Digital Transformation, IoT, and AI Convergence

Over the past decade, three powerful forces have been quietly aligning—digital transformation, the Internet of Things (IoT), and artificial intelligence. Each one on its own has reshaped parts of the business landscape, but together, they're creating something exponentially more powerful. Their convergence isn't just driving change; it's laying the foundation for how modern enterprises think, act, and compete—and digital twins sit right at the intersection.

Digital transformation used to mean putting processes online or shifting data to the cloud. Today, it's about building organizations that are responsive, data-driven, and ready for what comes next. It's no longer just about efficiency—it's about visibility, resilience, and the ability to adapt in real time. Companies are moving beyond digitizing documents or modernizing software. They're rewiring how their systems talk to each other, how decisions are made, and how quickly they can pivot when the unexpected happens.

IoT has accelerated this shift by giving the physical world a digital voice. Sensors are now embedded in everything—from machines and vehicles to buildings, supply chains, and even human bodies. These devices generate an overwhelming amount of real-time data about location, temperature, vibration, pressure, movement, usage, and more. But data alone doesn't change anything—it's the ability to interpret and act on it that makes the difference.

That's where AI steps in. Artificial intelligence transforms raw data into insight. It detects patterns, predicts outcomes, and recommends actions that human teams might miss. It enables digital twins to become intelligent companions—ones that not only reflect the present, but also anticipate the future. Through machine learning and analytics, AI allows a digital twin to recognize anomalies, simulate scenarios, and optimize performance on its own.

When these three technologies converge, the result is a real-time, learning system that connects the physical and digital worlds in ways we've never had access to before. Imagine a manufacturing line where machines communicate their needs, adjust based on incoming materials, and alert operators to issues before they arise. Or a hospital where patient data flows from wearable devices to digital models that help doctors make faster, more precise decisions.

This convergence isn't theory—it's already happening. And it's accelerating. The companies that are embracing this shift are discovering a new kind of visibility into their operations—one that doesn't just inform them of what's happening but empowers them to act faster, smarter, and more confidently. Digital twins are the vehicle through which this convergence becomes usable, scalable, and deeply transformative.

External Pressures: Sustainability, Regulation, Cost-Cutting

No business operates in a vacuum. Every industry today is feeling the squeeze of external pressures—some subtle, some impossible to ignore—all pushing companies to rethink how they operate, spend, and grow. Sustainability, rising regulatory demands, and relentless cost-cutting are no longer edge considerations. They're front and center. And they're not going away.

Sustainability isn't just a buzzword—it's become a business imperative. Consumers expect environmentally responsible practices, and investors are backing organizations that can prove they're serious about their environmental, social, and governance (ESG) commitments. That means less waste, lower emissions, more transparency, and smarter use of resources. But meeting those expectations requires more than good intentions. It demands real-time insight into how energy is used, how materials flow, and where inefficiencies are hiding. Digital twins provide that visibility. They allow companies to simulate the impact of changes before acting, optimize resource use, and track performance down to the micro level. It's not just about compliance—it's about building smarter, cleaner systems that can evolve.

Then there's regulation, tightening across almost every sector. Governments are imposing stricter controls on safety, emissions, data privacy, traceability, and ethical sourcing. Staying compliant is no longer a periodic box-checking exercise—it's a constant, dynamic requirement. Digital twins make it possible to monitor, document, and report operations with precision. They create a living audit trail and allow businesses to adapt quickly when rules change. Whether it's tracking food safety in supply chains or managing carbon outputs in manufacturing, the ability to stay ahead of compliance issues becomes a strategic edge.

And of course, there's the bottom line. Cost pressures are unrelenting. Materials are more expensive, energy prices are volatile, and customers expect faster delivery at lower prices. Businesses are expected to do more with less—without sacrificing quality. That's where digital twins step in as a cost-cutting force multiplier. They allow organizations to reduce physical prototyping, avoid unplanned downtime, fine-tune operations, and make better decisions faster. By catching problems before they escalate and revealing opportunities that would otherwise go unseen, digital twins drive efficiency not just on paper, but in action.

Together, these external pressures are rewriting what it means to be competitive. The businesses that thrive are the ones that can respond to complexity with clarity, to pressure with precision. Digital twins don't just help companies react—they help them stay a step ahead.

Growing Need for Predictive, Not Reactive, Decision-Making

The old way of doing business relied heavily on reacting. A machine breaks, and you fix it. Sales dip, and you investigate. A delay hits the supply chain, and teams scramble to patch things up. It's a cycle of chasing problems after they've already done damage. But in a world moving this fast—where every second of downtime costs money, every misstep risks trust, and every delay affects the bottom line—reactive decision-making just doesn't cut it anymore.

Businesses today need foresight. They need systems that can recognize patterns, anticipate disruptions, and guide smarter decisions before issues ever surface. That's where digital twins show their true power—not as a tool for reacting to problems, but as a platform for predicting and preventing them.

With real-time data flowing in from sensors, machines, environments, and people, digital twins can identify subtle shifts that signal a future problem. A rise in vibration here, a dip in pressure there—tiny changes that might go unnoticed by human eyes but tell a clear story when processed through AI and machine learning. This kind of predictive insight allows businesses to intervene early, adjust course, and avoid costly breakdowns.

But it's not just about maintenance. Predictive decision-making spans every corner of operations. Forecasting demand more accurately. Identifying process bottlenecks before they slow production. Rerouting deliveries ahead of weather disruptions. Understanding how a small tweak in one system could ripple across the entire business. These aren't just convenience features—they're critical capabilities in an increasingly complex and high-pressure landscape.

The truth is, no one can afford to rely solely on past data anymore. The conditions of yesterday don't guarantee the outcomes of tomorrow. To compete today means understanding what's coming, not just what's already happened. Digital twins provide that forward-facing lens. They turn raw data into foresight. They let you simulate choices, weigh options, and see outcomes before they hit your real-world operations.

And when decisions are made from that place—not from reaction, but from readiness—businesses become not just more efficient, but more resilient. They're not waiting for impact. They're already adjusting, already optimizing, already moving forward.

The Rise of Virtual-First Development

There was a time when physical prototypes were the gold standard—build it, test it, fix it, repeat. It was the way products were designed, factories were planned, and systems were launched. But that method is expensive, slow, and increasingly out of sync with the demands of today's fast-moving markets. In its place, a new approach has taken hold: virtual-first development.

Virtual-first doesn't mean abandoning the physical—it means flipping the process. Instead of starting with tangible assets and reacting to real-world outcomes, businesses now begin in the digital world, where ideas can be tested, pushed, and perfected without risk. Digital twins make this shift possible. They allow teams to model complex machines, entire workflows, and even human behavior in environments that replicate reality with stunning accuracy.

With physics-based simulations and real-time data inputs, companies can explore multiple designs or production setups without ever touching a physical component. They can see how a machine behaves under load, how a new process affects efficiency, or how a product performs in different conditions—all before investing a dollar in materials or labor. This isn't theoretical—it's happening in industries like manufacturing, where companies using Mevea's digital twin platform have drastically reduced the number of prototypes they need. And it's happening in healthcare, where virtual organs are used to simulate procedures or predict patient outcomes.

Virtual-first development isn't just about speed, though it delivers that in spades. It's about confidence. When teams can explore "what if" scenarios in a safe, digital environment, they don't just move faster—they make better decisions. And when those decisions are backed by data, simulation, and continuous feedback, the leap from concept to execution becomes smoother, smarter, and far less costly.

This approach also opens the door to broader collaboration. Stakeholders no longer have to wait for a prototype to see what's coming. Engineers, designers, operators, and even customers can interact with a digital version of a product or system early in the process, offering input that improves the outcome. It's more agile, more inclusive, and far better suited to a world where innovation can't wait for trial and error.

In a virtual-first world, development doesn't slow down to catch up with the physical—it brings the physical up to speed. Digital twins are what make that possible. They allow companies to create, test, and iterate at the pace of imagination, without sacrificing precision or performance. It's not the future of development. It's the new standard.

Industry Urgency: Disrupt or Be Disrupted

There's a quiet race happening across industries right now—one that doesn't always make headlines, but is already reshaping who stays competitive and who falls behind. The rules of business are being rewritten by speed, intelligence, and adaptability. And at the heart of it is a stark choice: disrupt or be disrupted.

Digital twins have become one of the clearest indicators of where that line is being drawn. Early adopters are already using them to reduce waste, predict failures, and streamline operations in ways their competitors can't match. They're not just gaining efficiency—they're changing expectations. They're delivering better products, faster services, and smarter experiences. And once customers, partners, or markets get a taste of that level of performance, they don't go back.

That pressure is being felt across every sector. In manufacturing, legacy systems that once held up fine are now struggling to keep pace with the agility of smart factories. In healthcare, hospitals that rely solely on traditional diagnostics risk falling behind as personalized, data-driven care becomes the norm. Even in urban planning, cities that don't adopt digital twins for traffic, energy, and infrastructure management are watching smarter cities take the lead on sustainability and livability.

The threat isn't just falling behind—it's becoming irrelevant. Competitors who understand their operations in real time, who can test ideas before implementation, and who catch issues before they become problems, will always move faster and smarter. They'll bring products to market quicker. They'll reduce costs with precision. They'll build trust with consistency. Meanwhile, companies still stuck in reactive, disconnected systems will find themselves scrambling to catch up.

This urgency isn't fear-mongering—it's reality. And the beauty of digital twins is that they don't just help you keep up; they give you the tools to lead. To see further. To act faster. To adapt smarter. For businesses today, the decision isn't just whether to invest in digital transformation. It's whether to do it before someone else redefines the market you thought you understood.

Disruption isn't a wave that might come someday. It's already moving. The only question is whether you're riding it—or getting swept under.

Case Studies: Shanghai's Digital City, Amazon Go Stores

Some of the most compelling evidence for the power of digital twins doesn't come from theory—it comes from what's already happening on the ground. Two standout examples, Shanghai's digital city and Amazon Go stores, show just how differently the world can function when physical systems are mirrored, analyzed, and optimized through intelligent digital replicas.

Shanghai has built what is arguably one of the most ambitious digital twins in the world: a real-time, data-rich replica of the entire city. It's more than just a map. This digital twin models traffic flow, monitors waste disposal, tracks public utilities, and provides insights that allow city officials to simulate and test decisions before making them in the real world. It's like having a city-sized video game, but the outcomes directly impact millions of people's lives. If planners want to reroute traffic, change delivery zones, or adjust energy distribution, they don't have to guess. They run scenarios inside the digital twin to see exactly how those changes would play out—then implement the best option with confidence.

This kind of city-scale visibility isn't just impressive—it's transformative. It means Shanghai can respond to emergencies more effectively, use resources more efficiently, and plan for future growth in ways that are smarter and safer. It also sets a new benchmark for what urban management can look like in the digital age. As more cities follow suit, this level of responsiveness and intelligence will shift from groundbreaking to expected.

On the other end of the spectrum—but just as revolutionary—is Amazon Go. These checkout-free retail stores operate on an ecosystem of sensors, cameras, and AI-powered digital twins. Every product, shelf, and customer is tracked in real time. As someone walks into the store, picks up items, and leaves, their actions are recorded and interpreted by a digital system that understands exactly what's happening, where it's happening, and when. No scanning, no lines, no friction. The digital twin of the store is aware of both the physical inventory and customer behavior at every moment.

This model doesn't just offer convenience—it fundamentally redefines the shopping experience. It reduces labor costs, eliminates bottlenecks, and provides a rich layer of behavioral data that Amazon can use to improve layout, product placement, and customer engagement. It also changes expectations. Once people get used to walking out of a store without stopping at a register, waiting in line starts to feel outdated.

Both of these examples highlight different ends of the digital twin spectrum—macro and micro, public and private—but they share a common theme: awareness leads to better action. Whether managing a metropolis or optimizing a retail experience, digital twins provide the clarity and confidence to make smarter decisions in real time. And for businesses watching from the sidelines, these aren't just impressive case studies—they're signals of what's coming next.

Digital twins have stepped into the spotlight not because the technology suddenly appeared—but because the world changed around it. The need to predict instead of react, to optimize instead of overspend, to adapt instead of stall—that need is now urgent. And the businesses that understand this shift are the ones rewriting the rules. They're not just digitizing. They're simulating, learning, improving—in real time. That's the new standard. Not transformation someday, but intelligence now. Because the future isn't waiting. And neither should you.

Chapter 3

Common Misconceptions (And Why They Matter)

It's easy to misunderstand digital twins. The term itself sounds slick and futuristic—like something meant for cutting-edge tech labs or billion-dollar enterprises. For many, it gets lumped in with the endless wave of digital buzzwords that promise transformation but rarely deliver. Others mistake it for a fancy 3D graphic, a costly gimmick, or something too complicated to implement without overhauling everything. These misconceptions might seem harmless on the surface, but they carry weight. They quietly shape decisions, stall innovation, and cause businesses to underestimate what digital twins are actually capable of. And in doing so, they leave value on the table.

Misunderstanding a technology this powerful doesn't just slow adoption—it blinds companies to the opportunities they're already equipped to take. To move forward with clarity and confidence, these myths need to be dismantled. Because once you see what digital twins really are—and just as importantly, what they're not—everything else starts to come into focus.

"It's Just a CAD Model"

One of the most common misconceptions about digital twins is that they're just glorified CAD models—slick 3D renderings with no real depth or function beyond looking impressive. This misunderstanding isn't surprising. After all, digital twins do often include 3D visualizations, and many people's first exposure to them comes through highly polished marketing videos or product demos showing smooth, rotating models on a screen.

But the truth is, that visual component—the CAD-like appearance—is just the surface. A digital twin is not about how something looks; it's about what it knows and what it does. A CAD model is static. It's a design file created at a single moment in time, often before the product or asset even exists. It doesn't change, it doesn't learn, and it doesn't reflect real-world conditions. It's a blueprint—useful for design and planning, but blind to what's actually happening once the product is in use.

A digital twin, by contrast, is alive. It continuously ingests data from sensors, systems, and software connected to its physical counterpart. It evolves with every shift in temperature, vibration, usage, or location. If a component begins to fail, the digital twin reflects that degradation in real time. If the environment changes—say, increased load on a system or unexpected usage patterns—the twin adapts its model accordingly. It's a dynamic, context-rich representation that mirrors the behavior, performance, and condition of the real-world asset across its lifecycle.

To put it another way, a CAD model tells you what something is supposed to be. A digital twin tells you what it's actually doing right now—and what might happen next. That's a massive leap in capability.

Intel's work in spatial digital twins illustrates this perfectly. Their system doesn't just create a model of a factory floor—it maps the positions of machines, people, and cameras in real time. It understands where each object is and how it's behaving in relation to everything else. It's this layer of spatial intelligence, fused with real-world sensor data, that allows the twin to predict collisions, optimize movement, and maintain safety without human intervention.

Meanwhile, in the healthcare space, researchers aren't using CAD files to predict a heart attack—they're using data-driven digital twins of actual human hearts. These models aren't designed for looks. They're built from MRI scans, genetic data, and real-time biometrics, simulating blood flow, stress, and electrical activity. They change with the patient. They learn. They respond. No CAD model could come close to that level of intelligence or personalization.

So yes, digital twins might include a visual component. But to reduce them to just a 3D model is like calling a smartphone a "digital clock" because it tells time. You're missing the power that lies underneath.

The danger of this misconception isn't just technical—it's strategic. When business leaders dismiss digital twins as superficial, they overlook their potential to drive real outcomes. They see a fancy visual and assume it's marketing fluff, not a tool that could reduce downtime, improve quality, prevent failure, or save lives.

To move forward, companies need to stop thinking of digital twins as digital drawings and start seeing them for what they really are: intelligent systems that bridge design, operation, and insight. It's not the image on the screen that matters—it's the data behind it, and the decisions it helps make.

"You Need Expensive Hardware to Start"

Another widespread myth about digital twins is that they require a massive upfront investment in high-end hardware to even get started. It's the kind of assumption that stops decision-makers in their tracks. They picture fleets of cutting-edge sensors, advanced robotics, custom-built infrastructure, and cloud computing costs piling up—and understandably, they hesitate. The idea that digital twins are only for big-budget companies with deep tech stacks and endless resources is not just misleading—it's outdated.

The truth is, the barriers to entry have dropped significantly. Yes, early implementations of digital twins were hardware-heavy and resource-intensive. In those early days, the concept was mostly confined to aerospace programs and advanced manufacturing floors, where budget constraints were less of a concern and the payoff of precision justified the cost. But today's reality is different. Now, many businesses already have the foundational tools in place—they just haven't connected them.

The first step to building a digital twin doesn't require tearing down your infrastructure or buying exotic equipment. Often, it starts with data you're already collecting. Most modern facilities already use IoT-enabled devices, smart sensors, and programmable logic controllers. These systems generate streams of valuable information—temperature, motion, vibration, flow, location—but that data is often underutilized or locked in isolated systems. A digital twin simply brings that data into a unified, intelligent model where it can be put to work.

Consider the example of Mevea. Their software doesn't demand that companies build physical replicas or buy specialized hardware before creating digital twins of heavy machinery. Instead, it uses existing product designs and control system data to simulate performance with high accuracy. Their physics-based modeling tools allow companies to test and refine machines before anything physical is produced. The savings come not from fancy gadgets, but from reducing waste, eliminating costly prototypes, and identifying problems early.

Intel's scenescape platform follows a similar principle. It uses off-the-shelf cameras and sensors, many of which businesses already have installed, to create spatial awareness and track movement in real time. What makes it powerful isn't the hardware—it's the software that interprets, correlates, and contextualizes the data. You don't need a new fleet of devices. You need a smarter way to use the ones you already have.

Even cloud infrastructure, which once posed significant cost hurdles, is now scalable and flexible enough to support digital twin deployments at almost any level. Many platforms offer pay-as-you-go models, making it possible for businesses to start small—monitoring a single process, machine, or site—and scale up as they prove value.

This myth is dangerous not because it's completely false, but because it's exaggerated to the point of inaction. It convinces teams they're not ready when they are. It holds back innovation under the assumption that digital twins are a luxury, not a necessity. But in reality, smart implementation often starts with minimal upgrades and a clear strategy.

The businesses making real progress in this space aren't the ones with the flashiest tools—they're the ones who understand their data, connect their systems, and start where the opportunity is biggest. Sometimes that's a high-precision factory. Sometimes it's a retail space. Sometimes it's a city block. And sometimes, all it takes is a few connected devices and a willingness to think differently.

Digital twins aren't about how much tech you own. They're about how intelligently you use what you've already got.

"Only for Manufacturing"

One of the most limiting misconceptions about digital twins is that they're only useful in manufacturing. The assumption here is that the value of digital twins is confined to production lines and heavy machinery—industries where the impact of failure can be costly, and efficiency is paramount. While it's true that manufacturing was one of the earliest industries to adopt digital twins, this narrow view overlooks the breadth of their applications across virtually every sector.

The truth is, digital twins have proven invaluable in fields that stretch far beyond the factory floor. The idea that they are only for manufacturing stems from the early adoption of the technology in product design, testing, and process optimization. In these environments, digital twins serve as a mirror for machines, helping to predict failures, optimize operations, and enhance safety. But over the years, this technology has evolved, and its benefits have extended into numerous other industries.

Healthcare is one prime example. Digital twins of organs, systems, and even individual patients are already being developed to model health conditions and predict outcomes. By simulating a person's heart, doctors can predict the likelihood of heart disease based on their unique biometrics. In surgery, digital twins allow doctors to rehearse procedures in a virtual setting, improving precision and minimizing risk. This is not science fiction—it's a growing reality, with applications ranging from personalized treatment to medical research.

In urban planning, digital twins are transforming how cities are managed. Cities like Shanghai have built real-time digital replicas of their infrastructure, providing city planners with a dynamic view of everything from traffic flows to waste management. This helps them plan infrastructure upgrades, optimize transportation routes, and even test emergency response strategies—all in a virtual space before any physical work is done. It allows for more intelligent, data-driven decision-making at a scale and speed that wouldn't be possible otherwise.

Energy and utilities are also embracing the power of digital twins. Energy companies are using digital replicas of their grids to better understand demand, predict outages, and optimize distribution. By analyzing real-time data from thousands of sensors across the network, companies can foresee potential problems before they become full-blown outages. In renewable energy, digital twins of wind turbines, solar farms, and even entire energy systems help improve efficiency, reduce maintenance costs, and increase uptime.

The retail industry has also found value in digital twins. Amazon's Go stores are a clear example of how digital twins are revolutionizing retail experiences. Through real-time tracking of customer movement, product placement, and even inventory management, Amazon

Go's systems ensure a seamless, frictionless shopping experience. Retailers also use digital twins to simulate store layouts, optimize product placement, and even predict customer behavior based on foot traffic patterns.

Even agriculture is being transformed by digital twin technology. Farms are using digital replicas of crops, irrigation systems, and soil conditions to predict yields, optimize water usage, and monitor plant health. Digital twins help farmers make smarter decisions about planting schedules, resource allocation, and pest control, ultimately improving productivity and sustainability.

The misconception that digital twins are only for manufacturing limits their potential. The truth is, any industry that deals with systems, assets, people, or processes can benefit from digital twin technology. Whether you're managing a city, running a hospital, or optimizing a supply chain, a digital twin offers a more accurate, data-driven way to understand what's happening now, anticipate future scenarios, and make smarter decisions.

Digital twins are versatile tools, applicable to virtually any business or operational environment. The key is understanding their capacity to simulate, predict, and optimize—not just in factories, but across industries that require real-time insight and intelligent decision-making. The technology has matured, and its applications are only expanding. The question is not whether digital twins are for your industry, but rather how soon you can start using them to transform your operations.

The Cost of Misunderstanding: Missed Value and Fragmented Systems

Misunderstanding what digital twins truly are—and what they can actually do—doesn't just slow down adoption. It actively costs businesses in ways they may not even realize. When leaders reduce digital twins to little more than flashy visuals or assume they're too complex or niche for their operations, they're missing out on measurable, strategic value. They overlook opportunities to reduce waste, prevent failure, improve safety, and accelerate innovation. And worse, they often invest in fragmented technologies that fail to deliver the bigger picture.

The most immediate consequence of this misunderstanding is missed value. Without a clear understanding of how digital twins function as real-time, decision-driving systems, businesses fall back on outdated methods: reactive maintenance, trial-and-error prototyping, manual oversight, and siloed data analysis. Each of these costs time, money, and efficiency. Digital twins, when implemented correctly, replace guesswork with precision. They enable you to model complex behavior before committing resources, predict outcomes instead of waiting for failure, and connect data streams to form a cohesive, actionable view of your operations.

Take Mevea, for example. Their approach to digital twins emphasizes early-stage simulation—building a physics-based model of a machine before it's ever physically constructed. This allows companies to run thousands of real-world scenarios virtually, testing durability, responsiveness, and environmental conditions without ever cutting metal. The result? Fewer prototypes, faster development cycles, and massive savings in materials and engineering hours. For companies stuck in the old assumption that digital twins are just 3D models for visual reviews, this kind of value is completely invisible—and therefore, unattainable.

Another cost of misunderstanding is fragmented systems. When digital twins are mistaken for isolated tools—like separate monitoring dashboards, isolated AI models, or simple automation scripts—organizations tend to deploy technology in silos. One team uses vision systems for quality control. Another tracks energy usage. A third installs motion sensors for safety. Each of these systems may function well on its own, but without a digital twin strategy to unify them, they can't collaborate, share context, or optimize collectively.

This is where Intel's scenescape platform shines. Rather than treating sensors, cameras, and AI as standalone tools, scenescape combines them into a spatially aware digital twin of an environment. For example, in a factory, it doesn't just detect that a person or object is present. It knows exactly where it is, when it appeared, and how it's moving in relation to machines, robots, or safety zones. It brings spatial intelligence into machine decision-making—something a patchwork of individual systems can't do alone.

Imagine a scenario where a robot is coming around a blind corner and a person is walking toward the same spot. In most factories, the security camera might record it. The safety sensor might catch the movement. But unless those systems are part of a unified digital twin that understands spatial context, the robot won't slow down in time. That's the risk of fragmented systems—they see slices of reality, not the whole picture. A digital twin connects those slices into something actionable.

Beyond safety, this interconnected view opens the door to cross-functional optimization. Operations, maintenance, logistics, and planning teams can all work from the same real-time source of truth. When data flows into a central, intelligent model, insights multiply. Decisions improve. And the organization moves from putting out fires to designing better systems altogether.

Misunderstanding digital twins also leads to underutilized data. Many businesses already collect vast amounts of data but don't know how to extract real value from it. Without a twin to contextualize, interpret, and simulate that data, it stays trapped in databases and dashboards. It's like owning a thousand puzzle pieces but never assembling the picture.

Digital twins turn those pieces into a living map—one that doesn't just describe the past, but guides the future.

Both Mevea and Intel prove that digital twins are not just about tech—they're about strategic clarity. They make the invisible visible, the complex manageable, and the disconnected unified. But none of that happens if they're misunderstood or underestimated. To capture the full power of digital twins, organizations must see them not as optional add-ons, but as core infrastructure for how modern businesses operate, adapt, and grow.

The cost of getting it wrong isn't just a missed opportunity—it's a competitive disadvantage. In a landscape where speed, intelligence, and resilience are everything, misunderstanding digital twins is a luxury no business can afford.

Clearing up the confusion around digital twins is more than a technical correction—it's a strategic shift in mindset. When you stop thinking of digital twins as static visuals or overly complex systems, and start seeing them as flexible, living tools that connect data, context, and real-world impact, the potential becomes undeniable. These aren't abstract concepts or tools reserved for tech giants. They're accessible, practical, and already reshaping the way modern businesses operate. The sooner these myths are put to rest, the sooner companies can stop hesitating—and start building smarter.

PART II

HOW DIGITAL TWINS WORK

Chapter 4

Foundations of a Digital Twin System

Beneath every high-functioning digital twin lies a foundation of systems working in harmony—sensors feeding streams of real-world data, intelligent models processing that information, and platforms stitching it all together into something that actually makes sense. From the outside, a digital twin might look seamless. But behind the scenes, it's a finely tuned engine built on precise data, smart connectivity, and rock-solid structure. It's not magic. It's architecture—and understanding how that architecture works is key to unlocking the full power of a digital twin. Without the right foundations, what looks like a twin is really just a digital shell. But when all the pieces come together, it becomes something alive—something that sees, learns, and responds in real time.

The Core Building Blocks of a Digital Twin

What gives a digital twin its edge—its ability to perceive, adapt, and even anticipate—isn't any one piece of technology. It's the harmony between several essential components, each doing its part to bring a digital model to life. These aren't just technical details tucked away in the background—they're the heartbeat of the entire system. When these building blocks work together, a digital twin becomes more than a replica. It becomes a dynamic, decision-making environment that transforms how businesses operate in the real world.

Sensors and IoT: Giving the Physical World a Voice

The starting point of any digital twin is the physical asset itself—be it a machine, a room, a production line, or a human body. But it's the sensors attached to that asset that give it a digital voice. These sensors track everything from motion and vibration to temperature, humidity, pressure, speed, and flow. They transform physical changes into data points, and in doing so, they become the nervous system of the digital twin.

Enter the Internet of Things (IoT), the network that connects these sensors and allows them to communicate in real time. It's through IoT that raw data flows from the edge—factories, equipment, buildings—into centralized systems that can interpret and act on that information. Without IoT, data stays locked in individual devices. With it, the physical world becomes part of a much bigger, smarter conversation.

This is what allows digital twins to respond as conditions evolve. A slight increase in motor vibration, a shift in air quality, or a delay in machine response time becomes a signal, not just an isolated event. The twin sees it, contextualizes it, and helps decision-makers (or autonomous systems) understand what it means and what should happen next.

The beauty is that most businesses already have some form of this infrastructure. Machines come equipped with basic diagnostics. Buildings have HVAC monitors. Vehicles have GPS and onboard diagnostics. The raw ingredients for a digital twin are often already there—it's the orchestration that brings them to life.

Real-Time Data Collection: The Lifeblood of the Twin

While sensors generate the data, it's the flow of that data—accurate, continuous, and time-aligned—that gives the twin its pulse. Real-time data collection is what separates a digital twin from a static model or a periodic snapshot. It allows the digital representation to evolve in sync with its real-world counterpart.

But this isn't just about speed—it's about precision. A digital twin thrives on reliable, time-stamped inputs. When multiple data streams—from vibration sensors, cameras, location trackers, and control systems—are coming in at once, they need to be synchronized. Without it, the digital model can drift from reality. If the temperature reading is delayed by a few seconds or a location signal is off by a meter, decisions based on that data may be flawed.

Consider a warehouse where autonomous robots navigate in tight spaces. If the location data from one robot lags, the system might assume it's in a different place, creating a risk of collision. Real-time data doesn't just improve performance—it ensures safety, efficiency, and accuracy across every layer of operation.

Moreover, the value of real-time data is not only in what's happening now, but in how it informs the next moment. When trends emerge, anomalies surface, or predictive thresholds are crossed, the system can respond immediately. That responsiveness is what gives digital twins their edge. It's what turns data into action, and systems into strategy.

Simulation Engines: Predicting the Future Before It Happens

At the heart of a digital twin's intelligence is its simulation engine. This is where data is transformed into insight. Simulation engines take the information flowing from the physical world and use it to model behavior, test outcomes, and run "what-if" scenarios in a risk-free environment.

This isn't hypothetical modeling done once during the design phase—it's continuous simulation, recalibrated by live data. Think of a product being tested against thousands of stress conditions—not in a lab, but virtually, while it's already in use. Think of a factory line where you can test five different process changes before implementing a single one. That's the power simulation engines deliver.

Companies like Mevea lead in this area, providing physics-based digital twins that simulate machinery behavior under a wide range of conditions. These engines allow engineers to test machines before they're built, explore how systems react to real-world forces, and refine performance without waiting for failures to happen in the field.

But simulation is more than just risk mitigation—it's strategic exploration. It enables businesses to innovate faster, optimize continuously, and move from reactive problem-solving to proactive design. Whether simulating human movement in a retail space, traffic flow in a smart city, or energy consumption in a data center, these engines empower digital twins to not just reflect reality—but improve it.

Integration Platforms: Connecting It All Together

None of this works without a strong integration platform. A digital twin is only as smart as its ability to connect with the systems and tools around it. Integration is what turns scattered devices, isolated data, and independent processes into a unified, functional whole.

Integration platforms are responsible for data orchestration, system interoperability, and seamless communication across technologies. They allow a digital twin to pull data from enterprise systems like ERP or MES, communicate with cloud analytics platforms, and interact with control systems on the edge. Without this layer, the data remains fragmented, insights remain buried, and the twin remains incomplete.

This is also where standards like USD (Universal Scene Description) and GLTF (Graphics Language Transmission Format) come into play. These frameworks, often borrowed from the gaming and design worlds, provide structure for how environments, objects, and systems are modeled digitally. Intel, for instance, has leveraged standards like these to build

Scenescape—a platform that doesn't just collect and display data, but aligns it spatially and temporally to reflect real-world behavior.

Integration is also what allows scale. It ensures that a digital twin built for one machine can eventually be expanded to represent a process, then a system, and eventually an entire operation. It allows businesses to grow their digital twin strategy incrementally, building on what they have rather than starting from scratch.

When all four of these building blocks—sensors and IoT, real-time data collection, simulation engines, and integration platforms—are in place and working together, the digital twin transforms from a technical project into a strategic asset. It becomes the lens through which businesses can not only see their operations but understand them. Optimize them. And reinvent them.

And this is just the beginning. Because with a solid foundation in place, digital twins are no longer confined to theory or small-scale pilots. They become living systems that evolve, expand, and adapt—right alongside the businesses they serve.

The Importance of Unit Standardization (SI Units)

In the world of digital twins, where precision is everything and countless systems must work in perfect sync, there's one foundational principle that often gets overlooked: standardizing the way we measure things. It may sound basic, even mundane, but without unit standardization, a digital twin can't function with accuracy, reliability, or clarity. In fact, without it, the entire system risks falling apart before it even starts.

To understand why this matters so much, consider what a digital twin is really doing. It's not just collecting raw data—it's turning that data into a real-time, actionable replica of the physical world. That means it has to know exactly how far something is, how hot, how fast, or how much force is being applied—not just in abstract terms, but in consistent, universally understood units. One system might report a length in meters, while another reports it in inches. One sensor might track weight in pounds, another in kilograms. Unless all those inputs are aligned under the same measurement system, the digital twin can't paint an accurate picture. It's like trying to assemble a puzzle with mismatched pieces—it just won't fit.

The problem isn't just theoretical. It's happened in very real, high-stakes scenarios. One of the most famous examples is NASA's Mars Climate Orbiter, a $327 million spacecraft that was lost because one team used imperial units (pounds of force) and another used metric units (newtons). The spacecraft didn't know the difference—and as a result, it disintegrated upon entering Mars' atmosphere. The lesson? Even the most advanced systems can fail if they don't speak the same language.

Now apply that principle to a smart factory, a fleet of autonomous vehicles, or a hospital filled with interconnected devices. If temperature readings are coming in Fahrenheit but your analytics engine is expecting Celsius, the system could misinterpret normal readings as dangerous—or vice versa. If camera data describes distance in pixels while the robot it's guiding expects millimeters, you could end up with misalignments, collisions, or flawed automation. These aren't just annoyances—they're real risks to safety, efficiency, and performance.

This is why SI units—the International System of Units—matter so much. They provide a universal framework for measurement that removes ambiguity and ensures compatibility across systems. By defaulting to SI units like meters, kilograms, seconds, and degrees Celsius, digital twin systems ensure that every input, every output, and every simulation is operating on the same foundation. It's the invisible glue that holds the entire ecosystem together.

Intel's digital twin work reflects this need for rigorous unit standardization. When modeling environments for spatial awareness and real-time object tracking, every input—from camera pose to object movement—must be mapped in the same coordinate system with consistent units. A bounding box around a moving vehicle, for example, means nothing unless the system knows where that camera is, how it's oriented, and how its field of view translates to real-world distances in meters—not just pixels. If those units aren't consistent, the model breaks down. The data becomes useless, or worse, misleading.

In Mevea's case, physics-based simulation of heavy machinery demands high fidelity. The software must know exactly how weight, torque, pressure, and motion interact. That level of realism is only possible when everything is calculated using the same unit base. You can't simulate how a machine will respond to stress or heat if your inputs are inconsistent or uncalibrated. Precision demands a shared standard—and SI units provide that common ground.

Even outside the digital twin itself, unit standardization is critical for integration. Enterprise systems—like ERP, supply chain tools, or maintenance platforms—often come from different vendors, built on different assumptions. Without a unified measurement standard, trying to connect them into a seamless digital twin is like plugging in electronics with incompatible voltage. You might get data, but you won't get insight.

Unit standardization also lays the groundwork for automation. In a future where machines talk to machines and make decisions in real time, there's no room for ambiguity. A robot can't ask for clarification. A machine learning algorithm won't raise a red flag if it receives measurements in feet instead of meters—it will simply calculate based on faulty assumptions. That's why consistency isn't just helpful—it's non-negotiable.

In the end, building a digital twin without unit standardization is like constructing a skyscraper on sand. It might look stable at first, but as you add complexity, everything becomes more fragile. The more systems you connect, the more important it becomes that every part speaks the same measurement language.

So while it might not be the flashiest part of the digital twin conversation, standardizing units is one of the most essential. It's what makes everything else possible—simulation, prediction, automation, safety, and trust. Without it, the twin isn't a twin at all. It's a fragmented illusion, vulnerable to error and built on miscommunication. But with it, the digital twin becomes something solid. Something dependable. Something ready to operate at scale—with clarity, confidence, and control.

Coordinate Systems and the Role of Spatial Mapping

To truly understand how digital twins function—not just in theory, but in the real world—you need to grasp the silent architecture that holds it all together: coordinate systems and spatial mapping. These aren't flashy, and they rarely make it into headlines. But without them, a digital twin is blind. It might know that something is happening, but not where it's happening or how it relates to everything else around it. And when the goal is to mirror the physical world with precision, location is everything.

Imagine a smart warehouse. Sensors pick up a worker walking through an aisle, a robot transporting goods, and a conveyor belt operating nearby. Each sensor sees part of the picture. But unless the system understands where those sensors are placed, how they're oriented, and what direction they're facing, it can't piece those signals together into a full, coherent view. It might know there's motion in "Camera 3," but without spatial context, that means almost nothing. Is that person near an active machine? Are they approaching a blind corner? Is the robot's path about to intersect with theirs? Without a shared coordinate system, there's no way to know.

That's why spatial mapping is such a critical function of digital twins. It provides the digital twin with a consistent frame of reference—anchoring every sensor, camera, and data stream to the same physical reality. It transforms data from disconnected sources into a living, navigable map. One that doesn't just tell you what's happening, but where, how, and what it means.

At the core of this lies the coordinate system. Much like GPS uses latitude and longitude to define positions on Earth, coordinate systems in digital twins define the spatial relationship between every element in a space—machines, people, infrastructure, even air flow. Whether using global coordinates (in geospatial applications like smart cities) or local ones (for indoor environments like factories or hospitals), the key is consistency. Every object and sensor must report its data in a common spatial language so that the digital twin can interpret it correctly.

Intel's scenescape platform is a real-world example of how this plays out. The platform maps out environments in 3D, assigning coordinates to every device and creating a shared understanding of space. When a person or object is detected by a camera, scenescape doesn't just record it—it places it within a virtual model of the environment, showing exactly where it is, how it's moving, and what it might interact with next. This spatial awareness is what allows intelligent systems to prevent accidents, reroute autonomous robots, or optimize foot traffic in real time.

Without spatial mapping, you might have a dozen cameras capturing movement in a facility, but you'd still be stuck watching feeds manually, trying to figure out what's happening where. With spatial mapping, those same cameras become part of an intelligent system that understands space. It can track motion through different areas, predict paths, flag anomalies, and respond without human input.

Coordinate systems also play a vital role in fusing data from different sensor types. A camera might provide visuals. A LIDAR sensor might give point clouds. A temperature gauge adds thermal data. Spatial mapping integrates all of this into one layered, coherent environment. It's not just data—it's data with context. That's the difference between a camera that sees an object and a digital twin that knows what the object is, where it is, and why it matters.

Consider the analogy of a security system with multiple Ring cameras. As a human, you can stitch together the feeds because you know your home's layout. But to a computer, "Camera 1" and "Camera 2" are just labels. Unless the system knows the physical orientation and position of each camera, it can't understand how one view connects to the next. Spatial mapping teaches the system to "see" space the way we do—intuitively and relationally.

In smart cities, the same principles apply on a larger scale. Shanghai's digital twin doesn't just monitor data points—it maps waste management routes, traffic flows, energy distribution, and pedestrian behavior in one cohesive environment. It lets city planners simulate and test decisions in a fully mapped-out cityscape—because understanding where something is happening is often the first step in knowing what to do about it.

Coordinate systems also support scale. A digital twin that accurately models a single room today can, through proper spatial architecture, grow to include an entire building, then a facility, then a network of facilities. When every part of the system shares a common spatial framework, expansion becomes seamless instead of chaotic. And as operations become more complex, that consistency becomes essential to keeping everything aligned.

Without spatial mapping, a digital twin is just a fragmented view of isolated systems. With it, it becomes a true reflection of physical space—a place where virtual intelligence can monitor, simulate, and influence the real world with awareness and precision.

In short, spatial context turns data into decisions. It connects the dots between motion and meaning, location and logic, cause and effect. And for a digital twin to be more than a model—for it to think, act, and adapt in the real world—it needs to understand where things are. Because only when everything is in place can the system truly come to life.

Challenges of Integrating Diverse Data Sources & The Physics-First Mindset: From Pixels to Meters

One of the biggest promises of digital twins is their ability to unify data—from machines, systems, environments, and people—into a single, intelligent model. But that promise doesn't come without serious complexity. In reality, integrating data from diverse sources is one of the most demanding aspects of building a digital twin. It's not just about collecting the data. It's about aligning it, cleaning it, translating it, and making it make sense—all in real time.

Think about the different types of data a digital twin might need to work with: video from cameras, numerical data from temperature sensors, accelerometer readings, RFID scans, log files, GPS signals, pressure gauges, digital forms, user inputs—the list is endless. Each one comes in a different format, at a different frequency, with its own naming conventions, units of measurement, and spatial reference frames. Some are structured, others are messy. Some stream in milliseconds, others are batch processed in hours. It's like trying to have a meaningful conversation in a room where everyone is speaking a different language, at different speeds, and referring to different maps.

This is why the challenge isn't just technical—it's architectural. If systems aren't aligned from the ground up, the digital twin quickly becomes a fragmented mess. You might have excellent insights in one part of your operation, but no way to link them to another. You might know the pressure in a pipe, but not its location. You might have machine vision identifying objects, but no connection to spatial awareness or motion data. Disconnected data is data without meaning. It might tell you what is happening, but not where, why, or what to do about it.

This is where the physics-first mindset comes in—a principle that both Intel and Mevea emphasize in their approach to building digital twins. Instead of focusing on abstract pixels or disconnected readings, a physics-first mindset grounds everything in real-world units, real-world motion, and real-world behavior. It treats every piece of digital data as a shadow of something physical—something that has mass, energy, force, direction, and time.

Let's start with the basics: most visual sensors—like cameras—see the world in pixels. They know that an object appears at coordinate (240, 380) in the frame, or that a person's outline has shifted slightly from one frame to the next. But pixels don't exist in the real world. You can't measure distance in pixels. You can't make safety decisions or machine adjustments based on screen coordinates. What you need is a translation—from pixels to meters. From 2D screen space to 3D physical space.

Intel's scenescape tackles this by anchoring every sensor and data stream to a shared spatial model. Cameras aren't just collecting images—they're tagged with their exact position, orientation, and field of view in the environment. When a person is detected in a frame, scenescape can calculate their real-world location, movement trajectory, and relationship to nearby equipment or zones. This allows the system to move beyond "what's in the camera view" and answer questions like: Is that person about to enter a restricted area? Are they in the path of a robot? Should the system intervene?

This isn't possible without a physics-first approach. It requires not just seeing the object, but understanding where it is, how it's moving, and what physical laws apply. It's a shift from interpreting the world visually to understanding it spatially and physically—like a human brain, but faster and more precise.

Mevea, on the other hand, applies this philosophy from a simulation standpoint. Their platform doesn't just animate machines for demonstration—it simulates their real-world behavior using the same laws of physics that govern their performance in the field. Mass, torque, friction, inertia—these aren't afterthoughts. They're baked into the digital twin's core. This allows engineers to run highly accurate tests on machines before they're even built, using digital twins that react to real-world forces as if they were the physical object itself.

This is where the two philosophies—Intel's spatial intelligence and Mevea's physics simulation—converge. In both cases, data isn't treated as an isolated stream. It's connected to something tangible, something measurable, something real. And this connection creates the foundation for deeper insight, more accurate prediction, and safer, smarter automation.

But make no mistake: getting here isn't easy. Integrating diverse data sources still requires serious engineering. It means translating between formats, building APIs, resolving timing mismatches, and cleaning dirty data. It means developing common reference models, defining metadata standards, and investing in interoperability.

Yet, the companies that embrace this challenge head-on are the ones that unlock the real magic of digital twins. They move past isolated dashboards and into unified environments where every signal tells a story—and where every story leads to smarter decisions.

In the end, the real strength of a digital twin isn't its complexity—it's its coherence. And coherence starts with alignment. Alignment between systems, units, timeframes, and dimensions. When you take a physics-first mindset, and you connect every stream of data to a real-world anchor, you don't just create a digital model—you build a digital reality. One that mirrors the physical world not just in form, but in function. One that learns, adapts, and moves with it—every second, in perfect sync.

A digital twin isn't a single tool or system—it's an ecosystem. Its strength comes not from any one part, but from how all the parts work together: physical sensors, digital models, real-time feedback, contextual awareness, and intelligent decision-making. When the foundation is solid—when data is structured, systems are connected, and information flows with purpose—a digital twin becomes far more than a mirror. It becomes a partner in performance. A second mind for your operations. And it's from this foundation that smarter strategies, safer environments, and faster decisions begin to take shape.

Chapter 5

From Data to Decision–The Intelligence Layer

Raw data, on its own, is just noise—numbers without meaning, signals without purpose. Businesses today are collecting more data than ever before, but the real value doesn't lie in the volume. It lies in what you can do with it. That's where the intelligence layer of a digital twin comes into play. It's the part that thinks, that learns, that connects dots and turns information into action. This layer is what separates a digital twin from a data warehouse or a static dashboard. It's not just about storing or visualizing data—it's about interpreting it in context, predicting what comes next, and guiding decisions that are faster, smarter, and more confident.

Data Processing, Context Building, and AI/ML

The strength of a digital twin isn't just in its ability to mirror the physical world—it lies in how intelligently it can interpret what it sees. That interpretation begins with data, but it doesn't end there. Data, after all, is only as useful as the meaning we can extract from it. What elevates a digital twin beyond a basic monitoring tool is its capacity to process raw input, layer on context, and apply intelligence through artificial intelligence (AI) and machine learning (ML). This is the heartbeat of the intelligence layer—and it's where data transforms into action.

From Raw Streams to Useful Signals

Every sensor, camera, and device in a digital twin ecosystem is constantly producing data. But raw data doesn't arrive neatly packaged. It's fragmented, noisy, and often unstructured. A vibration sensor might generate a thousand readings per second. A camera might capture movement but not understand what it's looking at. A temperature reading might show fluctuation, but without context, there's no way to know if that's normal or dangerous.

The first step in making sense of this deluge is data processing. This includes filtering out noise, removing redundancies, smoothing signals, and organizing information into meaningful formats. For instance, when Intel's Scenescape platform ingests footage from multiple cameras, it doesn't just stack the footage—it aligns it, tags it with metadata, and synchronizes it in time and space. That's how it becomes possible to say: "This person entered here, moved this way, and will likely end up over there."

Data processing is the cleansing and organizing step. But it's only the beginning.

Context: The Missing Piece

What really makes data valuable is context. It's not enough to know that something happened—you need to know what it means. A vibration reading of 0.02 might signal a problem in one machine, but be perfectly fine in another. An object appearing in a camera feed might be a security threat in one scenario, or just normal traffic in another. Without context, even the most accurate data can be misinterpreted—or ignored.

Digital twins excel at building this context. They connect data to physical models, environmental conditions, historical trends, and spatial relationships. They don't just say "a machine is running hot." They say, "Machine A is running 6 degrees hotter than usual, after a maintenance delay, in an area with limited airflow, while operating under higher-than-average load." That level of insight isn't possible from a single data source. It requires layered understanding—and that's what context delivers.

Mevea's simulation tools take this further by embedding physics into the context. The platform doesn't just simulate how a machine moves—it understands why it moves that way under stress, torque, or load. That physical intelligence, combined with real-time data, builds a rich, accurate model of how the system behaves—and how it's likely to respond to future changes.

AI and Machine Learning: Turning Patterns Into Predictions

Once data is processed and contextualized, the real intelligence begins. This is where artificial intelligence and machine learning step in, helping the digital twin not just reflect reality, but learn from it.

AI algorithms comb through vast amounts of incoming data to detect patterns, flag anomalies, and make correlations that human analysts might miss. Machine learning models take this a step further by improving over time—adapting to new behaviors, refining predictions, and becoming more accurate with every data cycle.

Let's say a machine starts vibrating at a slightly unusual frequency. On its own, that might seem insignificant. But an ML model that's been trained on months or years of similar data might recognize it as an early sign of component fatigue—long before human operators or rule-based systems would notice. That insight can trigger a preemptive maintenance action, saving time, cost, and possibly preventing a catastrophic breakdown.

In healthcare, AI-enhanced digital twins can monitor patient data and predict deterioration hours—or even days—before symptoms become visible. In logistics, they can forecast supply chain disruptions based on weather, traffic, or inventory fluctuations. In retail, they can analyze shopper movement to optimize store layouts and personalize experiences.

These are not just analytics. They're decisions waiting to be made. And they're made faster, more accurately, and more consistently when backed by AI.

Crucially, the most effective digital twins combine rule-based logic (for predictable scenarios) with machine learning (for complex or evolving ones). This hybrid approach allows businesses to maintain control while benefiting from adaptive intelligence. You define thresholds, alerts, and business rules—but the AI watches for what you didn't know to look for.

And perhaps most importantly, these systems improve with use. The longer a digital twin runs, the more data it collects, the smarter it gets. It begins to anticipate failure, forecast demand, and optimize performance without constant reprogramming. Over time, it becomes less of a tool and more of a strategic advisor—offering insight that's grounded in real-world behavior and sharpened by continuous learning.

In the end, data alone doesn't change anything. It's the ability to interpret that data, in context, with intelligence, that turns information into impact. And that's the job of the intelligence layer—taking raw streams and transforming them into a living, learning system that doesn't just watch what's happening, but helps decide what should happen next.

Temporal and Spatial Awareness

For a digital twin to function as more than just a fancy data dashboard, it needs to understand not only what is happening, but when and where it's happening. These two dimensions—temporal (time-based) and spatial (location-based) awareness—are what give a digital twin its depth. They're what allow it to track movement, predict behavior, detect collisions, optimize workflows, and uncover patterns that would otherwise remain invisible. Without them, you're just looking at disconnected data points. With them, you're seeing a real-world system unfold, evolve, and respond in real time.

Let's start with temporal awareness—the understanding of when events occur, how long they last, how they relate to each other in time, and what that timing reveals. In a digital twin, every data point is stamped with time. That seems simple, but it's crucial. Timing gives context. A vibration spike in a machine could be meaningless—or it could be the moment just before a critical failure. If that spike happened during startup, it might be normal. If it happened mid-cycle, it might be cause for concern. The difference lies in the when.

This becomes even more critical when data from multiple systems is combined. If a robot arm pauses for two seconds, a conveyor belt slows by half a meter per second, and a camera picks up a shadow in the same zone—all at the same time—the twin can infer a real-world interaction. But if those events are out of sync by just a few seconds, the connection might be missed entirely. That's why precision time-stamping is essential. It allows systems to correlate actions and reactions accurately, forming a cohesive story of what's happening across the environment.

In industrial settings, temporal awareness enables smarter scheduling, predictive maintenance, and event reconstruction. If something goes wrong, the system doesn't just show the outcome—it can replay the chain of events leading up to it. In healthcare, it can track changes in patient vitals over time to spot deterioration.

In supply chains, it can monitor how long goods sit idle and how that affects freshness, cost, or risk. In every case, timing transforms static data into a living timeline of insight.

Now layer on spatial awareness—the ability to understand where things are, how they move, and how they relate to the space around them. This is where digital twins step into the physical world. They don't just receive data—they place that data within a 3D map. They know where machines are located, where people are walking, where cameras are positioned, and how all of these elements interact within the same coordinate system.

Intel's scenescape is built around this principle. It doesn't just recognize that an object appeared in a camera's field of view—it knows exactly where that object is in the real world. It knows the camera's pose, its field of view, and how that translates to real-world coordinates. It turns image pixels into spatial coordinates. From there, it can track movement across zones, understand proximity to hazards, and even predict the next move based on direction and velocity. That's spatial awareness at work.

When you combine temporal and spatial awareness, digital twins can go far beyond basic monitoring. They can simulate interactions, predict conflicts, and even automate safety responses. For example, if a worker steps into a zone that a robot is about to enter, the digital twin can recognize the overlap in both time and space—and trigger an emergency stop. Not after the fact. Before impact.

This combination also enables path prediction. If a person is walking down a hallway and disappears from one camera, the system can estimate when and where they'll reappear next, based on their last known speed, direction, and environmental layout. If they don't reappear on time, that gap can signal a deviation or a potential issue. In this way, the twin doesn't just respond to movement—it anticipates it.

In logistics, spatial-temporal awareness helps optimize flow. If trucks are arriving too close together at a loading dock, causing bottlenecks, the system can adjust schedules in advance. If certain warehouse aisles consistently have overlapping traffic patterns, layout changes can be tested digitally before making real-world adjustments.

And in environments like hospitals, the ability to track people, equipment, and assets in both space and time can improve everything from patient safety to operational efficiency. Want to know how long a patient waited between check-ins? Where critical instruments went missing? How long a room stayed idle after discharge? The digital twin knows—because it remembers both where and when.

Ultimately, temporal and spatial awareness is what turns a digital twin from a passive observer into an intelligent, responsive system. It enables the twin to recognize patterns, detect risks, and make connections that are invisible to systems operating in flat timelines or isolated spaces. It turns raw data into movement, story, cause and effect. And when time and space come together in real-time simulation, businesses gain something incredibly powerful: not just awareness, but foresight. The ability to see what's coming—and to act before it happens.

The "What, Where, and When" Triad of Sensor Intelligence

At the heart of every high-functioning digital twin is one fundamental principle: clarity. The system must know what's happening, where it's happening, and when it's happening. That simple triad—What, Where, and When—is the backbone of sensor intelligence. It's how raw data becomes real-time understanding. And without all three working together, a digital twin can't deliver the deep insight or predictive power it's built for.

Start with the "What". This is the core of object recognition—identifying what the system is looking at or detecting. Is it a person? A vehicle? A box? A conveyor belt? This is where traditional AI and machine learning models, like computer vision or object detection algorithms, play a major role. A camera may detect movement, but AI determines that the movement is a forklift, not a human. Or that the pattern on a product surface indicates a defect.

The "what" is essential, but on its own, it's shallow. Knowing what was detected doesn't help much if you don't also know where it is.

That's where the "Where" comes in. This isn't just the most overlooked piece of the triad—it's often the most misunderstood. In sensor systems, knowing that an object exists means very little unless you can locate it with precision in the physical world. A bounding box around a person in a video feed is great—but unless the system knows where the camera is mounted, how it's angled, and how that view maps to a physical space, it can't place that person in the real environment. And if it can't place them, it can't make intelligent decisions about interactions, safety, or behavior.

This is where spatial mapping and coordinate systems step in. The digital twin must translate visual data into measurable, physical distances. That means turning pixels into meters, direction into vectors, and screen space into real-world context. Without that, a machine might know "a person is present," but not whether they're in a restricted area, approaching an operating robot, or just walking down a hallway.

Now add the final piece: "When." Timing is everything. A system that doesn't understand time is always lagging behind—or worse, responding to things out of sync. When sensors operate at different refresh rates, or data arrives out of sequence, the digital twin can misread the situation entirely. It might think someone is standing in front of a robot when they've already moved. Or assume a door is still open when it closed five seconds ago. In environments like manufacturing floors, warehouses, or smart cities, that kind of error isn't just inefficient—it can be dangerous.

Precise, synchronized timestamping is what keeps the entire system grounded in reality. It lets the twin create a timeline of actions and events, identify cause and effect, and replay interactions to understand behavior and optimize future outcomes. It also allows systems to compare patterns over time—detecting when "normal" shifts subtly toward "problematic," even if the difference isn't immediately obvious.

When all three—What, Where, and When—come together, sensor data becomes something far greater than the sum of its parts. The system doesn't just see a person—it knows who, where they are, how they got there, and what might happen next. It can make real-time decisions, not just based on rules, but based on behavior.

Intel's Scenescape platform brings this to life. Its cameras and sensors work together not just to detect objects, but to locate them precisely and track them over time. That's how it creates spatially aware digital environments where machines and humans can coexist safely. A robot doesn't just avoid obstacles—it understands the context of movement around it and can slow down, reroute, or respond as needed. All of that is only possible because the system is fluent in the What, Where, and When of its environment.

The "What, Where, and When" triad also powers prediction. If you know what an object is, where it's located, and how fast it's moving, you can estimate where it will be—and when. That's how a digital twin anticipates a collision before it happens, or signals a process delay before it spirals into downtime. It doesn't just react to change. It stays ahead of it.

This triad also creates a foundation for deeper analytics. Over time, the system can track not just isolated events, but trends. It can ask: What tends to happen here at this time of day? Where are delays most common? When do maintenance issues typically arise? These questions don't have easy answers unless every piece of sensor data is anchored in time and space and tied to a clear understanding of the object or event involved.

In short, a digital twin that can't master the "What, Where, and When" is like a human trying to make decisions with blurry vision, no sense of direction, and no memory of the past. It might guess correctly now and then, but it won't be consistent, reliable, or strategic.

But when this triad is locked in—when every sensor input is processed with clarity, aligned with physical space, and grounded in time—the digital twin becomes a real intelligence layer. It doesn't just monitor. It understands. It doesn't just report. It guides. And in doing so, it turns the chaotic noise of data into a quiet, steady flow of insight that powers every decision forward.

Predictive Models: How They Learn and Act

If data is the lifeblood of a digital twin, then predictive models are its brain—the part that analyzes patterns, makes sense of complexity, and turns possibility into foresight. Predictive models are what make digital twins more than just real-time reflections. They give the system the ability to see ahead, to anticipate issues before they surface, and to recommend actions before problems escalate. And the most powerful part? These models get smarter the more they're used.

At the most basic level, a predictive model is a system trained to recognize patterns in historical data and use those patterns to forecast future outcomes. But the process isn't static or simplistic. These models are constantly evolving, thanks to advances in artificial intelligence (AI) and machine learning (ML). They don't just repeat what's been seen before—they learn, adapt, and improve with every data point they ingest.

Here's how the process works.

Step One: Feeding the Model

It starts with input. Predictive models require vast amounts of data to train. In the context of a digital twin, that data comes from every corner of the system—sensor readings, machine logs, maintenance records, human activity, environmental conditions, even external variables like weather or traffic. Every input adds a layer of nuance. A single vibration reading might not mean much on its own, but thousands of them over time begin to reveal patterns—how components wear down, how systems degrade, or how certain conditions trigger faults.

This data is processed, cleaned, and labeled to create the "learning set" that fuels the model. Historical patterns are mapped to outcomes. For example: "When temperature rises above X, and vibration reaches Y, failure occurs within 24 hours." The more examples it sees, the more accurate the model becomes.

Step Two: Learning the Patterns

Machine learning comes into play as the model begins to find statistical relationships within the data. It starts to understand not just individual variables, but how they interact. It learns that a minor pressure fluctuation might be irrelevant on its own, but when paired with a small drop in voltage and a slight delay in response time, it often precedes a failure.

This learning doesn't stop after the initial training. Modern predictive models use online learning—meaning they continue to refine their understanding as new data flows in. Every shift, every update, every unexpected event becomes a new datapoint to analyze and adapt to. Over time, the model doesn't just mimic human insight—it surpasses it, detecting relationships too subtle or complex for humans to catch.

Intel's Scenescape platform leverages this power by combining real-time environmental data with predictive intelligence. The system doesn't just recognize that a person is near a moving robot—it analyzes movement trends, predicts future positioning, and triggers safety protocols before paths intersect. The twin learns how people move through space, where bottlenecks form, and how to optimize for both safety and efficiency.

Step Three: Acting on Insight

Learning is only half the value of a predictive model. The real payoff comes in action—when the model's output is used to guide decision-making. That might mean triggering an alert, adjusting a process, delaying a task, or even automating a response entirely.

In manufacturing, a predictive model might recognize that a motor is on track to overheat based on current behavior and historical performance. It can recommend a cooldown cycle or schedule a maintenance check before damage occurs. In logistics, the model can predict delivery delays based on traffic, inventory status, and staffing patterns, and suggest rerouting to avoid disruption. In healthcare, it can forecast patient deterioration hours in advance, prompting proactive care that can save lives.

This predictive intelligence becomes even more powerful when combined with simulation. A digital twin can take the model's forecast, simulate several possible responses, and recommend the most effective course of action—before any real-world change is made. This gives teams the confidence to act, not just react.

From Prediction to Prevention

Predictive models don't just help organizations respond quickly. They help them respond early. And when you move from reaction to prevention, everything changes—costs go down, risks shrink, and operations run smoother. Downtime is minimized. Resources are used more efficiently. Customers receive better, faster service. And your teams gain more bandwidth to focus on growth, rather than firefighting.

Mevea's simulation-based digital twins push this even further by offering predictive models that are grounded in physical behavior. These aren't just statistical forecasts—they're simulations of what will physically happen under certain conditions. This kind of predictive modeling allows engineers to make precise adjustments to machines and processes long before a problem manifests in the real world.

Building Trust in the Model

One of the most critical parts of implementing predictive models is trust. People don't want to hand off decision-making to a black box. That's why the best digital twins are transparent—they don't just spit out a prediction, they show why the prediction was made. Which variables contributed. What pattern triggered the warning. How similar scenarios played out in the past.

This kind of explainability builds confidence—not just in the model, but in the decisions that follow. And when decision-makers trust the system, they're more likely to act early, consistently, and proactively.

A Learning System That Never Sleeps

In the end, predictive models turn a digital twin from a static reflection into a dynamic, forward-looking system. They bring a sense of time and anticipation to every decision. And because they're always learning, always adapting, they become more valuable with each passing day.

This is what makes digital twins truly transformative. They don't just answer the question, "What's happening now?" They answer, "What's likely to happen next—and what can we do about it before it does?" That's not just smart. That's strategic. And in today's fast-moving world, it's the difference between staying ahead—and getting left behind.

Case Study: Identifying Wear-and-Tear on Parts Before Failure & The Importance of Pose Detection and Camera Placement in Spatial Twins

One of the most tangible and business-critical use cases for digital twins lies in their ability to detect wear-and-tear on parts long before failure occurs. It's a quiet revolution happening behind the scenes—no headlines, no drama—just machines that run longer, safer, and smarter because the system watching them knows what's coming. And the reason it knows? A tightly orchestrated mix of real-time sensing, predictive modeling, and spatial intelligence—anchored by technologies like pose detection and strategic camera placement.

Let's start with a real-world scenario: a manufacturing facility running high-speed assembly lines, where motors, bearings, and joints operate under stress every minute of every day. In the past, wear would go unnoticed until something broke—causing costly downtime, safety risks, and a mad scramble to fix the issue. Preventative maintenance helped, but it was still a guessing game—servicing parts on a schedule, whether they needed it or not. It was wasteful, reactive, and often too late.

But when digital twins enter the picture, everything changes.

In this kind of environment, real-time monitoring through sensors captures vibration levels, temperature shifts, torque deviations, and even slight increases in resistance—each a subtle signal that something may be starting to degrade. On their own, these readings might seem insignificant. But fed into a predictive model trained on months (or years) of historical data, those patterns begin to reveal early-stage wear long before it becomes visible or dangerous.

The digital twin compares what's happening now to what should be happening, based on the known behavior of healthy parts. It looks for outliers, shifts, or combinations of symptoms that signal trouble. And when it spots something unusual—like a bearing vibrating at a slightly higher frequency under normal load—it doesn't wait for failure. It flags it, forecasts time-to-failure, and recommends an optimal intervention window. No panic. No surprises. Just smarter maintenance, fewer shutdowns, and major savings.

This predictive capability isn't just theory—it's actively being deployed. Mevea's simulation tools, for instance, allow manufacturers to model not only the mechanical behavior of components under stress but to test "what-if" scenarios around wear, fatigue, and heat buildup. Engineers can simulate how long a part will last under different loads or environmental conditions, all before a single real-world test. Combine that with data from the field, and you get a living, breathing maintenance strategy—one that adapts, learns, and evolves over time.

But predictive insight isn't just about what's happening—it's also about where and how. That's where pose detection and camera placement become game changers in spatial digital twins.

Why Pose Detection Matters

Pose detection refers to the system's ability to understand the orientation and position of objects—especially sensors and cameras—in physical space. This might sound like a minor detail, but it's foundational to spatial awareness. If a camera sees a person or machine part, but the system doesn't know the exact pose of that camera (its location, angle, tilt, direction), it has no way of translating that image into a real-world position. It's like seeing an object in a mirror without knowing where the mirror is—you lose all depth, direction, and spatial meaning.

Intel's Scenescape tackles this problem directly. Its spatial twins use precisely calibrated pose detection to map every camera, sensor, and object in a shared 3D coordinate system. This means the system doesn't just see motion—it understands it. It knows if a machine arm is moving out of alignment, if a person is standing too close to active equipment, or if two moving objects are on a collision path.

In the context of wear-and-tear, this matters because motion patterns tell stories. A tool that's slightly misaligned might still function, but over time, the irregular angle creates stress that accelerates breakdown. Pose-aware systems can detect this deviation early, even if the system is still technically "within spec." They see how the motion should look—and how it's starting to drift.

Strategic Camera Placement: Seeing the Right Things, the Right Way

Of course, even the best pose detection is useless if the cameras aren't placed thoughtfully. In spatial twins, camera placement is a design decision, not an afterthought. Each camera must be positioned to capture critical activity zones—equipment interaction points, safety areas, high-traffic paths—and calibrated to work in concert with other sensors in the environment.

If cameras are too high, too low, or at the wrong angle, the system might misinterpret depth, miss key interactions, or fail to track objects across zones. But when cameras are placed with spatial mapping in mind—angled to maximize overlap, minimize blind spots, and feed consistent data into the system—the twin becomes deeply aware. It can monitor everything from movement trajectories to zone violations to subtle misalignments that could indicate pending mechanical failure.

This spatial intelligence allows predictive models to factor in real-world geometry. For example, a part might wear faster when operating on a slope, or under certain rotational stress. A camera correctly positioned and pose-calibrated can capture the angle of operation, allowing the system to include those variables in its wear predictions.

And here's where it all connects: a digital twin that can see parts in real time, understand their spatial orientation, measure their performance through sensors, and predict their future state based on behavior is no longer just a monitoring tool. It's a preventative strategist. It's a quiet but constant guardian of uptime, safety, and cost-efficiency.

The Bigger Picture

When predictive maintenance powered by digital twins becomes the norm, the results ripple out. Equipment lasts longer. Maintenance windows shrink. Spare parts inventory becomes leaner and better timed. Unexpected downtime becomes rare. And over time, the system evolves—not just predicting failure, but learning how to avoid it altogether.

All of this depends on the right data. But even more critically, it depends on knowing what that data means in physical space and time. That's why pose detection and camera placement aren't just technical checkboxes—they're core components of intelligence. Without them, a digital twin is just watching. With them, it's understanding—and acting.

In the race to build smarter, safer, faster operations, the companies that invest in spatial awareness and predictive modeling won't just run more efficiently—they'll run circles around the ones that don't.

The intelligence layer is where a digital twin truly earns its value. It's what transforms data from passive observation into strategic foresight. With real-time context, predictive analytics, and adaptive learning, this layer becomes the brain behind the twin—an active partner in decision-making, not just a digital record-keeper. In a world that demands speed, resilience, and insight, it's no longer enough to know what's happening. Businesses need to know what will happen, why, and what to do about it. The intelligence layer delivers that clarity—and with it, a powerful edge in an increasingly complex world.

Chapter 6

Digital Twin Infrastructure & Ecosystems

Behind every digital twin that works flawlessly in real time is an invisible architecture—a network of platforms, protocols, and systems that must work in lockstep. It's not just about having the right sensors or the smartest algorithms. To build a digital twin that delivers consistent, scalable value, you need infrastructure that can handle the flow, processing, and orchestration of data across an entire ecosystem. This chapter looks under the hood—at the technical and organizational systems that make digital twins not just possible, but powerful. Because a twin is only as good as the ecosystem it lives in.

Interoperability: Making Systems "Speak the Same Language"

In the digital twin world, data is everywhere—flowing in from machines, sensors, IoT devices, legacy systems, cloud platforms, analytics tools, and more. Each one brings its own format, its own protocol, its own way of communicating. And while that diversity can be a strength, it also creates one of the biggest challenges in building a functioning digital twin: getting all these systems to talk to each other. That's the role of interoperability—the ability of diverse technologies to exchange data, understand it, and act on it as if they were built together from day one.

Without interoperability, a digital twin becomes fragmented. You might have high-quality data from your manufacturing line, but it can't sync with inventory updates from your ERP system. You might track human movement through cameras, but those systems can't interface with your safety automation tools. The result? Data silos. Operational blind spots. Missed insights. And a digital twin that never becomes truly "whole."

To solve this, organizations need to think beyond just collecting data. They need to focus on harmonizing it—building bridges between systems that speak different technical languages.

The Real Meaning of "Speaking the Same Language"

True interoperability goes deeper than simply linking APIs or setting up basic integrations. It means aligning on data formats, semantic meaning, units of measurement, time standards, and spatial frameworks. It means that when one system says "temperature," another system understands whether it's in Celsius or Fahrenheit—and knows what that reading applies to, where it was taken, and how recent it is.

It also means agreeing on data models—structured representations of physical systems, workflows, or processes. If every system models a machine differently, there's no shared understanding of what that machine is, what its parts are, or how it behaves. Interoperability requires a common language of objects, events, and relationships—one that systems can use to interpret and act on data without human intervention.

This is where standards come in—frameworks like USD (Universal Scene Description) or GLTF (Graphics Language Transmission Format) that define how scenes, objects, and data should be represented digitally. Originally developed for industries like gaming and animation, these standards are now being embraced by digital twin platforms as a way to align complex environments in a shared format.

Intel, for example, has leaned into this approach with Scenescape, using standard scene graph formats to represent spatial environments. This makes it easier to plug in new data sources, visualize them in consistent ways, and ensure that the system doesn't break when something changes. Instead of reinventing the wheel, Intel is building on battle-tested standards that were designed to scale.

The Hidden Costs of Incompatibility

When systems aren't interoperable, the effects ripple across the organization. IT teams spend countless hours building custom integrations that break every time something updates. Data analysts waste time converting formats instead of focusing on insights. And business leaders are forced to make decisions based on partial or outdated views of reality.

Worse, lack of interoperability limits the scale and adaptability of digital twins. What starts as a useful pilot can't expand beyond its silo because it wasn't designed to connect with other systems. You end up with multiple "mini twins" that don't talk to each other—each useful in its own right, but none capable of delivering enterprise-level intelligence.

In contrast, interoperable systems unlock agility. They allow companies to scale digital twins across sites, departments, and geographies. They let new technologies plug in with minimal friction. They support future-proofing—so when a new sensor, platform, or AI tool is introduced, it can join the ecosystem without starting over.

Building for Interoperability From the Ground Up

Achieving interoperability isn't something you bolt on after the fact. It's a mindset—a design principle that needs to guide decisions from day one. It means asking early questions like:

- What data standards do we need to adopt?
- How will our systems share time and location context?
- Can this new tool integrate with our broader ecosystem?
- Are we using open formats or locking into proprietary ones?
- How will this system evolve as new technologies emerge?

The answers to these questions shape not just the performance of a digital twin today, but its ability to grow and stay relevant over time.

The Human Element

It's worth noting that interoperability isn't just technical—it's organizational. Teams need to communicate as well as systems do. When departments use different platforms, measure success in different ways, or hoard data, even the most advanced tech won't bridge the gap. True digital twin success requires a culture of collaboration, transparency, and shared language—just like the systems that support it.

In the end, interoperability is about making your digital ecosystem coherent. It's about ensuring that every part of your infrastructure works together, shares understanding, and feeds into a larger intelligence. It's what transforms disconnected tools into a unified system. Data into insight. And digital twins into true strategic infrastructure.

Because the future of business isn't about who collects the most data—it's about who can connect it, understand it, and act on it—across every platform, process, and partner. That's the real language of progress. And it starts with making sure everyone—and everything—is speaking it fluently.

USD and GLTF: The Unsung Heroes of Digital Twin Interoperability

For a digital twin to function as a true mirror of reality—not just visually, but structurally and interactively—it must know how to represent the world around it in a way that other systems understand. It's not enough to have beautiful 3D visuals or accurate data inputs. What's needed is a shared format that allows different systems—whether they're from robotics, gaming, manufacturing, or urban planning—to work with the same model of the world. This is where two standards rise above the rest: USD (Universal Scene Description) and GLTF (GL Transmission Format).

You may not hear these names tossed around in boardrooms or strategy decks, but they're quietly enabling some of the most advanced digital twin ecosystems in the world.

What Is USD?

USD, or Universal Scene Description, was originally developed by Pixar to solve a very practical problem: how to manage incredibly complex animated scenes involving hundreds of assets, characters, lighting changes, and physics—all being worked on by teams across different locations and tools. They needed a way to describe a "scene" that was flexible, modular, and scalable—and most importantly, one that could be shared across diverse applications and workflows.

USD became exactly that. It's now the backbone for many industries that rely on high-fidelity 3D environments—film, design, simulation, and increasingly, digital twins.

Why? Because digital twins aren't just about a machine or a building. They're about environments—entire scenes that include machines, people, space, motion, and interactions. And USD doesn't just describe geometry. It handles:

- Hierarchical relationships (e.g., this motor is part of this machine, which sits on this floor, in this building).
- Variants (e.g., same model, different configurations).
- Time-based animation and change tracking (perfect for evolving, real-time twins).
- Layering and version control (allowing multiple systems to update or annotate the same scene without breaking it).

This is why companies like Intel are leveraging USD in platforms like Scenescape. When creating a spatially aware digital twin of a warehouse or city block, you don't just want to capture what's visible—you want to understand how everything relates. USD offers that depth, structure, and flexibility.

What Is GLTF?

GLTF, or GL Transmission Format, is another open standard—but it's built for speed, portability, and efficiency. Sometimes called the "JPEG of 3D," GLTF focuses on compact, efficient 3D asset exchange. It allows developers to render complex scenes quickly, with minimal computational overhead—perfect for real-time applications like AR/VR, web-based visualizations, and lightweight digital twins.

Where USD is ideal for complex, layered environments with rich metadata and dynamic behaviors, GLTF is better suited for performance-critical situations—say, viewing a machine model in a mobile app, or rendering product configurations in an online viewer.

GLTF supports:

- Meshes, materials, textures, lighting, and animations.
- JSON-based structure (lightweight and developer-friendly).
- Easy integration with WebGL, three.js, and other web visualization tools.
- Real-time rendering on devices with limited power (phones, tablets, browsers).

In a digital twin context, GLTF can be used to represent 3D objects that don't need the heavy overhead of simulation or behavior modeling—but still need to look and move realistically.

Why These Matter for Digital Twins

Digital twins rely on more than just visuals—they require a shared, extensible structure for describing physical environments in digital space. That structure must support different use cases, from high-performance simulations to accessible visualizations. It also needs to support integration across tools, vendors, and industries.

Both USD and GLTF answer that call, in complementary ways.

- USD is your deep, robust foundation—ideal for simulation, coordination, and collaboration in large, evolving scenes.
- GLTF is your portable, efficient format—perfect for visualization, sharing, and fast rendering.

Together, they form a critical piece of the interoperability puzzle—helping ensure that your digital twin doesn't get locked into proprietary formats or siloed ecosystems.

Real-World Impact

Let's say your factory is building a digital twin of its entire floor. Your machines, robots, cameras, and sensors are all mapped in a spatial environment. Engineers are using USD to model that environment and simulate workflows. Meanwhile, your operations team wants to view specific equipment in a lightweight web dashboard. They can use GLTF models of those assets, streamed directly into their browser or mobile device, without needing to load the full USD scene.

Or take a smart city project. Planners use USD to model traffic, infrastructure, and zoning logic, while emergency responders access fast-rendering GLTF views of city sectors to aid in response planning.

This flexibility—different layers of access, detail, and performance across teams—is only possible when you build on standards like USD and GLTF.

As digital twins grow in complexity and scope, the need for standardized scene representation will only increase. Whether you're modeling a single machine, an entire logistics network, or the layout of a global retail chain, the ability to speak a shared 3D language is what will determine whether your digital twin is truly scalable—or trapped in a vendor-specific silo.

USD and GLTF don't just make 3D data look good. They make it useful, portable, and collaborative. And in the evolving digital twin ecosystem, that might be the most valuable feature of all.

Gaming Industry's Contribution: Scene Graphs, Rendering Logic, and Physics

When people think of the gaming industry, they usually imagine immersive storytelling, stunning graphics, and addictive gameplay—not cutting-edge business technology. But behind the scenes, the technologies that power modern video games are increasingly fueling the rise of digital twins. Why? Because the gaming world has already solved some of the most complex problems digital twins now face—like building realistic virtual environments, simulating physics in real time, and coordinating dynamic systems across space and time.

As strange as it may sound, if you've ever watched a game character move seamlessly through a richly detailed environment—interacting with objects, responding to forces, and adapting to the player's input—you've seen the backbone of a digital twin in action. That backbone includes scene graphs, rendering logic, and physics engines—all of which are now being repurposed to model real-world environments in industrial, urban, and commercial settings.

Scene Graphs: The Hierarchy of Everything

At the heart of every modern game engine is a scene graph—a structure that represents all the objects in a 3D environment and their relationships to one another. It's like a digital family tree for everything in the scene. A lamp might be attached to a table. The table is inside a room. The room is inside a building. Move the table, and the lamp moves with it. That kind of nested, logical relationship is what makes scenes behave coherently.

Digital twins use this same logic to model real-world environments. For instance, in a digital replica of a warehouse, a conveyor belt has sensors, cameras, and moving parts. All of these elements must be represented as part of a unified system with defined spatial and functional relationships. A scene graph provides that structure. It tells the system not just what objects are present, but how they relate, what moves with what, and how interactions propagate through the environment.

Intel's use of scene graphs in its Scenescape platform shows how this concept enables spatial awareness and motion tracking. By mapping people, machines, and sensors into a structured 3D hierarchy, the system can understand behavior, detect risks, and manage interactions in real time. And it all starts with scene graphs—a core gift from the gaming world.

Rendering Logic: From Pixels to Perception

The second major contribution is rendering logic—the rules and algorithms that allow virtual scenes to be visualized with clarity, realism, and responsiveness. In gaming, rendering is designed to happen fast and efficiently, even on resource-constrained devices. This speed and visual fidelity is now being leveraged in digital twins, not just for aesthetics, but for usability.

When teams can explore a digital twin of a factory, city, or machine in real time—zooming in, rotating views, simulating changes—it helps them make better decisions. Engineers can visualize how a process will unfold. Maintenance teams can virtually inspect equipment before walking the floor. Executives can review layouts, traffic patterns, or structural changes without needing to be on site.

Standards like GLTF (also gaming-influenced) allow these environments to be rendered in browsers or mobile devices with low latency and high accuracy. The ability to see the digital twin in action, in a format that feels responsive and intuitive, increases adoption, comprehension, and confidence across every level of the business.

And just like in gaming, rendering logic supports layered visibility—meaning you can toggle on or off different views (e.g., sensor overlays, heatmaps, foot traffic, machine states), allowing users to customize the twin based on their role or task. This kind of interface fluency wasn't invented for industrial use—it was born in the world of games.

Physics Engines: Real-World Behavior in a Virtual World

Perhaps the most powerful contribution gaming has made to digital twins is the development of physics engines—the systems that simulate how objects move, collide, break, bounce, fall, and react to forces like gravity, friction, or torque. In a game, physics makes everything feel real. In a digital twin, physics makes everything behave real.

Platforms like Mevea harness advanced physics modeling to simulate machine behavior with stunning accuracy. It's not just about visualizing motion—it's about predicting stress under load, calculating fatigue over time, or modeling how a machine will respond to uneven terrain. This kind of simulation enables companies to test, validate, and refine products and systems before a single bolt is turned.

But again, the underlying tech? It's gaming DNA. Game developers have spent decades refining how to calculate interactions in 3D space without crushing performance. Now, that same logic is helping manufacturers predict failure, urban planners simulate traffic flow, and healthcare teams rehearse surgeries in virtual space.

Why It Matters

By building on gaming infrastructure, digital twins don't have to start from scratch. They can adopt battle-tested frameworks that are designed for interactivity, speed, and scale. More importantly, they inherit the mindset of simulation: test before you build, model before you deploy, and simulate before you commit.

This accelerates development, reduces cost, and dramatically improves decision-making. It also opens the door to real-time collaboration—where teams in different locations can interact with the same digital twin simultaneously, just like players in a multiplayer game. And with the rise of AR/VR, this immersive capability will only grow more powerful.

From Game Worlds to Real Worlds

The gaming industry didn't set out to build digital twins. But in solving the hardest problems of virtual environment design—like scene complexity, real-time rendering, and behavioral simulation—it created a foundation perfectly suited for the next wave of digital transformation.

Today, that foundation is being adapted and expanded, not just to entertain, but to engineer smarter systems, optimize real-world operations, and help people make better decisions in complex environments.

In short, the leap from gaming to digital twins wasn't accidental. It was inevitable. Because when you already know how to build entire worlds from code, applying that power to the real one is just the next logical step.

Real-Time vs. Latency-Bound Twins: The Verizon vs. Google Maps Analogy

Not all digital twins are created equal. In fact, one of the most important distinctions lies in how fresh the data is—how closely the digital model reflects what's happening in the real world right now. This leads to two broad categories: real-time digital twins and latency-bound digital twins. Understanding the difference between the two is essential when building or choosing the right kind of twin for your business.

And the best way to grasp that difference? Think of Verizon's real-time business infrastructure versus Google Maps.

The Latency-Bound Twin: Google Maps

Everyone uses Google Maps. It's powerful, intuitive, and helpful in countless ways. It gives you directions, shows you traffic patterns, offers satellite views, and even lets you "walk through" cities via Street View. But here's the catch—it's not truly real-time.

When you look at the front of your house on Google Street View, you're probably seeing a snapshot from months—or even years—ago. The cars in the driveway might not be yours. That tree in the yard? It might be gone now. Traffic conditions are often close to real-time, but even those are based on aggregated GPS signals and data that lag by a few seconds or minutes. This isn't a flaw—it's just the nature of how the system was designed.

Google Maps is a latency-bound digital twin. It gives a reasonably accurate, useful representation of reality—but not a live one. It's fantastic for planning, navigation, and general reference, but not ideal for making split-second operational decisions.

Many traditional industries operate with this kind of twin: monthly reports, historical dashboards, or periodic scans of equipment health. The system looks current, but it's always a few steps behind. Useful? Absolutely. But reactive, not proactive.

The Real-Time Twin: Verizon's Connected Intelligence

Now, flip to Verizon's approach to digital twins, particularly in enterprise infrastructure. Verizon is building real-time digital twins powered by 5G connectivity, edge computing, and live sensor data. These twins don't just reflect reality—they track it continuously. They're designed to respond, adapt, and update as events unfold, moment by moment.

Imagine a logistics center where a real-time digital twin monitors every package, vehicle, and human movement. If a forklift veers off course, the system flags it instantly. If there's a delay at a loading bay, the twin reroutes deliveries in real time. It's not looking at what was—it's tracking what is and predicting what will be. The decisions made here are based on now, not then.

Real-time twins are vital in mission-critical environments—manufacturing, healthcare, energy, smart cities—where timing and precision make the difference between efficiency and chaos, or even safety and risk.

Why the Difference Matters

The distinction between real-time and latency-bound twins isn't just academic—it has real consequences for how businesses operate and what they can achieve.

- Speed of Decision-Making: Latency-bound twins support long-term planning and analysis. Real-time twins enable immediate intervention.
- Risk Management: Real-time twins can prevent failures and accidents before they happen. Latency-bound twins can only analyze them after the fact.
- User Experience: Real-time data enhances automation, personalization, and responsiveness. Think smart stores, autonomous vehicles, or predictive healthcare.
- Cost Efficiency: Real-time systems catch inefficiencies as they occur, while latency-bound systems often uncover waste too late to recover.

That said, it's not a matter of one being better than the other. They serve different purposes. For instance, Google Maps is an extraordinary tool for strategic planning, route optimization, and geographic awareness. A latency-bound digital twin works well for historical analysis, trend forecasting, or design testing—where real-time data isn't critical.

But when your operations rely on split-second timing—such as preventing machinery collisions, rerouting vehicles, or adjusting to patient vital signs—you need a live, real-time twin. One that thinks fast, adapts fast, and acts fast.

Building for the Right Twin

The key for any business is knowing what kind of twin you need for each use case. Not every problem demands real-time intelligence, and not every environment can support it yet. Real-time twins require high-bandwidth data pipelines, edge computing resources, and robust sensor networks. That's why they're more complex to implement—but also more transformative when done right.

In contrast, latency-bound twins can be easier to deploy and still deliver significant value—especially when real-time insight isn't mission-critical.

In the end, it comes down to this: Do you need to know what happened, or do you need to know what's happening right now?

Digital twins can give you both. But only if you design your system to support the level of responsiveness your business actually needs. Choose wisely—and build accordingly. Because in the digital world, time isn't just money. It's intelligence. It's impact. And sometimes, it's everything.

Edge Computing vs. Cloud-Based Twins

& The Role of Network Infrastructure: Speed and Security as Enablers

When building and scaling digital twins, where data is processed matters just as much as how it's collected or displayed. At the heart of this infrastructure choice lies a pivotal trade-off: edge computing versus cloud-based twins. Each approach has its strengths, limitations, and ideal use cases. But no matter which path you take—or how you blend the two—there's one constant that underpins it all: your network infrastructure. Without fast, reliable, and secure connectivity, even the smartest digital twin is just an idea that can't execute.

Let's break it down.

Edge Computing: Fast, Local, and Responsive

Edge computing means processing data close to where it's generated—on or near the devices, sensors, or systems producing it. Think smart cameras in a factory, autonomous vehicles, or medical devices in a hospital. Rather than sending all that data to a distant cloud, edge systems analyze and act on it locally.

In digital twin terms, this enables real-time responsiveness. When milliseconds matter—like stopping a robot to prevent a collision or adjusting a machine's speed to avoid overheating—the edge wins. It eliminates the latency of routing data back and forth to the cloud and enables faster decisions at the point of action.

Imagine a warehouse floor where workers and robots share space. An edge-enabled digital twin processes camera feeds and sensor data in real time. It recognizes when someone steps too close to a moving vehicle and triggers a stop—not five seconds later, immediately. That kind of precision and reaction speed isn't just helpful. It's critical.

Advantages of edge-based twins:

- Ultra-low latency for real-time decision-making
- Local autonomy even during network interruptions
- Reduced bandwidth demands, as less data needs to be sent to the cloud
- Enhanced privacy, since sensitive data can be processed and stored locally

However, edge computing also has limitations. Local devices often have less computing power than cloud infrastructure. They may lack the ability to run complex simulations or store vast historical data. And they still need to be networked and updated securely—no easy feat when scaling across dozens or hundreds of locations.

Cloud-Based Twins: Scalable, Centralized, and Powerful

Cloud-based digital twins, on the other hand, aggregate and process data in centralized platforms—Amazon Web Services, Microsoft Azure, Google Cloud, and others. This model is ideal for system-level visibility, long-term trend analysis, and enterprise-wide coordination.

Take, for example, a logistics company managing hundreds of trucks across the country. A cloud-based twin can synthesize location data, traffic patterns, fuel consumption, and weather forecasts to optimize routing across the entire fleet. It's not about reacting in milliseconds—it's about orchestrating resources at scale.

In healthcare, a cloud-based digital twin might analyze patient data from multiple hospitals to identify population-level trends, improve diagnostics, or personalize treatment protocols using AI models too large to run on local devices.

Advantages of cloud-based twins:

- Scalable compute power for running simulations and training AI models
- Global data access across teams, sites, and systems

- Centralized updates and management
- Integration with enterprise systems (ERP, CRM, etc.)

But this model isn't without its weaknesses. Cloud twins can suffer from latency, network dependency, and data privacy challenges—especially when handling real-time interactions or sensitive environments.

Hybrid Approaches: The Best of Both Worlds

Smart organizations are increasingly adopting hybrid architectures, where edge and cloud work together. Edge devices handle time-sensitive tasks, while the cloud provides historical insight, broader coordination, and deeper analytics.

Intel's Scenescape is an example of this dual-layer strategy. Real-time tracking and spatial awareness happen locally to enable immediate responses. Meanwhile, higher-level processing—like pattern recognition, machine learning model updates, and long-term optimization—can be pushed to the cloud for scale and insight.

This balance allows digital twins to operate efficiently in the moment without sacrificing big-picture intelligence.

The Role of Network Infrastructure: Verizon's Edge

Whether you lean on edge, cloud, or both, the glue that holds everything together is your network infrastructure—and this is where companies like Verizon play a central role.

Digital twins are bandwidth-hungry, latency-sensitive systems. They require massive, continuous data flow, real-time communication, and ironclad security. A weak network turns a high-potential digital twin into a laggy, unreliable mess. But a fast, secure network becomes the backbone of a responsive, intelligent system.

Verizon's investment in 5G and private network infrastructure directly addresses these needs. With ultra-low latency, high throughput, and enhanced security, Verizon's networks enable real-time digital twins to function as they were meant to:

- In factories, robots and safety systems respond instantly to spatial awareness cues.
- In smart cities, sensor networks coordinate traffic, waste, and public safety dynamically.
- In healthcare, medical devices sync patient vitals with clinical systems in seconds, not minutes.

Security is equally important. Digital twins deal with sensitive data—from operational performance to personal health records. Verizon's secure networking solutions ensure that information flows safely across endpoints, protecting it from interception, corruption, or breaches.

Connectivity Is the Foundation

Ultimately, whether you're deploying a digital twin on the edge, in the cloud, or both, your network is the foundation. The most sophisticated models in the world won't work if they can't access timely data or communicate decisions fast enough to make a difference.

The future of digital twins lies in distributed intelligence—systems that think locally, learn centrally, and coordinate globally. That only works if the connections between those layers are seamless, fast, and secure.

And that's where infrastructure becomes more than tech—it becomes strategy. Because in a world that moves in real time, speed and security aren't just IT priorities—they're competitive advantages.

Digital twins don't exist in isolation—they thrive in connected ecosystems. Their true potential is unlocked when infrastructure is built not just to collect and store data, but to align it, scale it, and make it actionable across systems. The companies building real momentum with digital twins aren't just installing new tech—they're rethinking how their entire digital environment is structured. They're designing systems that are open, integrated, and ready to evolve. Because in a world where speed, precision, and insight drive everything, the strength of your infrastructure becomes the foundation of your advantage.

Chapter 7

Lifecycle of a Digital Twin

A digital twin isn't a static project you build once and forget. It's a living, evolving system—one that mirrors not just a moment in time, but an entire lifecycle. From early-stage design to real-world deployment, and from continuous monitoring to future upgrades, a digital twin grows and adapts alongside its physical counterpart. To unlock its full potential, you need to understand how it matures—what it needs at each phase, how it delivers value over time, and where the real inflection points occur. Because the most successful digital twins don't just reflect what is—they become a strategy for what comes next.

The Four Phases of a Digital Twin Lifecycle

A digital twin isn't just software—it's a dynamic representation of something real, built to live, learn, and evolve. And like any living system, it passes through distinct stages over time. Each phase in the digital twin's lifecycle brings new challenges, opportunities, and value. Understanding these four key phases—design and prototyping, deployment and monitoring, optimization and adaptation, and decommissioning and learning—is essential for getting the most out of your investment, both technically and strategically.

1. Design and Prototyping: Building the Blueprint Before Reality Exists

The lifecycle of a digital twin starts well before a product hits the production line or a building is constructed. It begins in the design phase, where the goal is to model the intended system in a virtual environment—long before it physically exists.

Here, the twin acts as a proving ground. It simulates how a machine, workflow, or process will function in the real world. Engineers test interactions, identify weaknesses, and experiment with different configurations—all without the cost or risk of building real prototypes. It's rapid iteration without material waste.

Mevea's physics-based simulation software is a clear example of this phase in action. Their twins don't just show what a machine will look like—they simulate real-world physics to understand how it will behave under pressure, load, and motion. Will this joint wear down after 1,000 hours? Will this arm fail when extended at full torque? These questions are answered in advance.

This phase saves time. It reduces the number of physical prototypes needed. It accelerates R&D. And perhaps most importantly, it allows stakeholders—from designers to decision-makers—to see, feel, and improve the system before any physical work begins.

2. Deployment and Monitoring: Going Live with a Digital Shadow

Once the physical system is built and put into operation, the digital twin evolves into a real-time reflection. Sensors begin streaming data into the model, enabling the twin to track performance, usage, and environmental conditions as they happen.

This is the phase where the twin becomes situationally aware. It starts to detect anomalies, track wear-and-tear, monitor energy usage, or predict failures before they happen. It may alert human operators, or in some cases, trigger autonomous responses.

In a factory setting, this might look like Intel's Scenescape mapping the exact location of workers, machines, and safety zones—instantly responding if someone enters a dangerous area. In healthcare, it could involve a digital twin of a patient's heart, updated with every new scan, showing how the organ is reacting to treatment in near real time.

Deployment also brings challenges: ensuring data flows cleanly from IoT devices, integrating with legacy systems, and making sure the twin maintains accuracy over time. Calibration and alignment matter. A small drift between the physical and digital models can compound into major misjudgments.

But when done right, this phase delivers visibility like never before. It closes the loop between intention and operation—bridging the gap between design and real-world execution.

3. Optimization and Adaptation: Learning, Evolving, Improving

Once a digital twin is actively monitoring its real-world counterpart, the next phase is all about refinement. This is where the twin shifts from mirroring the system to guiding its improvement.

The twin uses real-time data, historical trends, and machine learning to identify inefficiencies and recommend optimizations. It doesn't just highlight that something's wrong—it suggests how to make it better.

Maybe it finds a pattern in downtime that points to a process bottleneck. Maybe it detects excessive energy usage in a specific region of a facility. Maybe it learns to predict which machines need service before a scheduled inspection.

This phase is where predictive maintenance, AI-powered process tuning, and continuous improvement become real. The digital twin no longer just responds to problems—it helps prevent them. It becomes a performance coach, constantly searching for gains in speed, safety, cost, and sustainability.

It's also the phase where teams can simulate changes before rolling them out. Want to change a production workflow? Add a new conveyor path? Introduce a new robot? The twin can run the scenario, highlight risks, and show what's likely to happen—before anything is changed on the floor.

This continuous loop of feedback and refinement turns the twin into a living strategy engine—learning over time, adapting to new conditions, and growing more valuable the longer it runs.

4. Decommissioning and Learning: End of Life Becomes Start of Insight

Eventually, every physical system reaches the end of its life. A machine is retired. A building is closed. A product line is phased out. But in the world of digital twins, the story doesn't end there. The final phase—decommissioning and learning—can be just as powerful as the first.

Because the digital twin doesn't just disappear. It leaves behind a complete, time-stamped record of everything that's happened throughout the system's life: every input, every failure, every fix, every optimization. That dataset becomes a knowledge base—fuel for better design in the next cycle.

In this phase, the digital twin acts like a post-mortem analyst. It helps teams understand what went well, what didn't, and what could be improved in future designs. It can inform regulatory reporting, feed into predictive models for new systems, or even simulate what-if scenarios to explore alternative histories.

It also plays a role in sustainability. A well-maintained twin can help plan for material recovery, recycling, or responsible disposal—reducing environmental impact even at the end of life.

Decommissioning is often overlooked. But in a mature digital twin lifecycle, it's an essential phase—one that ensures every lesson is captured, and nothing is lost when the physical asset retires.

Together, these four phases form a continuous loop—not a straight line. Because every time a new asset is designed, it benefits from the insights of those that came before. Every twin informs the next. And over time, your organization moves from reacting to anticipating, from repeating mistakes to accelerating innovation.

That's the lifecycle of a digital twin: design it, deploy it, refine it, learn from it—and do it better the next time. Over and over again. Smarter, safer, faster.

Continuous Feedback Loops: The Self-Improving Engine of a Digital Twin

What truly sets a digital twin apart from traditional monitoring systems isn't just its ability to reflect reality—it's its ability to learn from it. At the heart of this intelligence is the continuous feedback loop, a cycle of real-time observation, analysis, action, and learning that never stops. This loop turns passive data into active insight. It powers adaptation, drives improvement, and gives the digital twin its ability to grow smarter with time.

A feedback loop might sound like a simple concept: you observe a system, compare it to expectations, and adjust based on the outcome. But inside a digital twin, this happens with high frequency, across multiple systems, involving complex interdependencies and machine learning. The result is a system that doesn't just watch—it evolves.

Observation: The Twin Watches Everything

It starts with observation—the digital twin constantly monitoring its physical counterpart through sensors, cameras, control systems, and user inputs. It watches how machines operate, how people move, how environments shift. Every vibration, temperature change, production cycle, or decision becomes a data point.

This raw stream of data is the fuel for everything that comes next. But it only becomes useful when the twin can place it in context—understanding what's normal, what's off, and what matters.

Comparison: Spotting the Gaps

Next, the system compares. Using baseline models, historical trends, and predictive analytics, the twin measures what's happening now against what should be happening. This is where anomalies are detected, trends are surfaced, and patterns begin to form.

Is this machine producing fewer units than usual during the same shift? Is foot traffic in a retail space lower than expected for this time of day? Are temperature levels trending upward beyond normal tolerances?

The twin doesn't just notice changes. It recognizes meaning behind those changes. It understands the cause-and-effect relationships that tie actions to outcomes.

Action: Make the Adjustment

When the twin detects something significant, it triggers action. This might be a real-time alert to a human operator, an automated system response, or a decision to initiate further simulation. The twin can recommend maintenance, reroute resources, slow down operations, or flag potential safety risks.

In more advanced systems, this action can happen autonomously—robotic arms adjusting their speed to avoid collisions, smart HVAC systems optimizing airflow based on occupancy, or delivery networks dynamically rerouting based on traffic and weather.

But the point isn't just to react. It's to feed those results back into the system.

Learning: Evolve the Model

Here's where the loop becomes powerful. After action is taken, the digital twin evaluates the outcome. Did the adjustment solve the problem? Did performance improve? Was the failure prevented?

This outcome is then fed back into the model, allowing the system to refine its algorithms, sharpen its predictions, and improve its accuracy. Over time, the twin doesn't just respond better—it anticipates earlier, acts faster, and becomes more precise.

Machine learning thrives in this environment. The more cycles the system runs through—observe, compare, act, learn—the more confident and capable it becomes. It starts to see problems forming long before humans do. It doesn't need to wait for failure. It prevents it entirely.

Across the Lifecycle: The Loop Never Ends

What makes continuous feedback loops so critical is that they function across every phase of the digital twin's lifecycle:

- During design, they help refine prototypes by simulating outcomes and incorporating test feedback.
- During deployment, they adjust system behavior based on real-world conditions and performance data.
- During optimization, they feed insight into machine learning models to improve predictions and efficiency.
- During decommissioning, they generate lessons that inform the next generation of designs.

These loops are never linear. They're recursive, real-time, and scalable. A digital twin with strong feedback mechanisms doesn't get outdated—it gets smarter. Every interaction, every exception, every decision becomes part of a growing intelligence.

And when feedback loops are shared across systems—when the twin of one machine informs the behavior of another, or when data from one facility trains the model for a new one—you get something even bigger: organizational learning at digital speed.

In a world where change is constant, complexity is rising, and downtime is costly, continuous feedback loops are the engine that keeps digital twins relevant, adaptive, and valuable. They don't just help you keep up—they help you stay ahead. Because when your systems learn faster than your problems evolve, that's when you stop reacting—and start leading.

Training via Simulation: Preparing People Through the Digital Twin

Digital twins aren't just transforming how machines operate—they're changing how people learn. One of the most practical, high-impact applications of digital twin technology is simulation-based training. By replicating real-world equipment, workflows, and environments in a virtual model, digital twins give operators, technicians, and frontline workers the chance to train, fail, and improve—before they ever touch the actual system.

In industries where mistakes are costly—or even dangerous—this is a game-changer.

From Classroom Theory to Hands-On Virtual Practice

Traditional training often separates learning from doing. Operators might watch videos, read manuals, or sit through presentations. But when they face the real equipment for the first time, it's often under pressure, with little room for error.

Digital twins collapse that gap. They turn training into hands-on simulation, mirroring not just the look of a system, but its behavior, logic, and feedback. Trainees can interact with the twin just like they would with the real machine—press buttons, move levers, monitor performance—and the twin responds with realistic physics and outcomes.

Need to practice restarting a stalled production line? Repairing a critical part? Navigating a high-risk scenario? The digital twin becomes your sandbox—a safe, repeatable, cost-free environment where you can build skills without fear of real-world damage.

Learning By Doing—Before the System Even Exists

This training doesn't need to wait until the physical system is built. In fact, it can begin during the design phase.

Mevea's simulation tools allow manufacturers to not only test machine performance during prototyping but to begin training operators before the first physical unit is assembled. That means staff are ready from day one—no learning curve, no delays.

This early-access training gives organizations a massive advantage. Instead of spending weeks onboarding new employees or retraining teams every time a process changes, digital twins allow learning to run in parallel with development. The moment the new system goes live, the people running it are already fluent.

Scenario-Based Training: Fail Safely, Learn Deeply

One of the most powerful uses of digital twin simulations is in scenario-based training. In these modules, workers are placed in realistic, sometimes high-pressure situations—emergencies, malfunctions, system failures—and must respond using the same tools and logic they would use in the real world.

Did they react fast enough? Did they follow the right sequence? Did they make a mistake—and if so, what were the consequences?

Because the simulation is built on real-world physics and logic, every outcome is believable. Every misstep carries weight. But no real damage is done. And that's the key: people can make mistakes, learn from them, and try again until they build not just competence—but confidence.

It's training that adapts to the learner's pace, provides instant feedback, and builds muscle memory long before there's a physical asset to touch.

AR/VR Integration: Immersive Learning Experiences

When paired with augmented reality (AR) or virtual reality (VR), digital twin training becomes even more immersive. Trainees can walk through a virtual factory, open up a digital engine, or rehearse a maintenance routine as if they were physically present. It's not just visual—it's spatial, interactive, and embodied.

This kind of training is especially valuable in industries like:

- Energy, where equipment is remote or dangerous
- Healthcare, where procedures are sensitive and time-critical
- Aviation, where pilots train for high-risk scenarios
- Manufacturing, where downtime is expensive and systems are complex

With AR/VR, a technician can learn to replace a faulty part without touching a single real component. They can rehearse the procedure over and over until it becomes second nature. And once they step into the real environment, their actions are faster, safer, and more precise.

Consistency, Scale, and Measurable Progress

Another key benefit of simulation-based training is standardization. Every trainee goes through the same scenarios. Every skill is assessed against the same benchmarks. That ensures consistent readiness across teams, departments, and locations.

And because the training lives in software, it scales easily. You don't need to build extra machines or tie up real-world systems. You just duplicate the twin—and train the next team.

Progress is measurable, too. Digital twins can track performance, spot areas of struggle, and personalize future training to focus on weak points. It's a feedback loop not just for machines—but for people.

Beyond Onboarding: Lifelong Learning in a Live System

Simulation isn't just for onboarding new staff. It's a tool for continuous upskilling. As systems evolve, processes change, or new technologies are introduced, digital twins let you update the training instantly—no downtime, no classroom needed.

And because the twin is always connected to the real-world system, training can be linked directly to live data. If a machine is showing signs of wear, the system could recommend refresher training for the team responsible. If a new procedure is launched, everyone can practice it in the twin before it hits the floor.

This keeps teams sharp, aligned, and confident—without waiting for mistakes to reveal the gaps.

Digital twins don't just train people—they empower them. They create a space where workers can learn without risk, fail without consequence, and grow without limits. In a world where change is constant and complexity is rising, this kind of training isn't a luxury—it's a competitive edge. Because when your people are prepared for anything, your systems are too.

Live Operational Insights: Seeing the Invisible in Real Time

One of the most valuable capabilities of a digital twin is its ability to give you a live window into how your operations are behaving right now. This isn't about reviewing what went wrong yesterday or looking at historical charts from last quarter—it's about understanding what's happening in real time, from the flow of people through a store to the energy consumption of a factory floor. Live operational insights transform business from a reactive game into a dynamic, responsive system.

And the beauty of it is—you're not guessing. You're seeing.

Footfall: Real-Time Human Movement

In retail, hospitality, transit hubs, or even office buildings, knowing how people move through a space has always been valuable. But with digital twins, this insight moves from guesswork or static heat maps to live, dynamic flow tracking.

Camera-based sensors and spatial mapping allow the twin to track how people enter, navigate, and interact with a space—down to specific zones or paths. Are there choke points? Are customers avoiding certain areas? Are foot traffic patterns shifting by time of day or promotional activity?

These insights let businesses:

- Optimize store layouts for better traffic flow
- Reduce wait times by adjusting staffing in real time
- Understand how people use public or private space over time
- Test design changes virtually before rolling them out physically

It's like installing a nervous system inside your building—constantly sensing, adjusting, and learning from movement.

Traffic: Smart Cities in Motion

Cities are living, breathing systems. Cars, pedestrians, bikes, delivery vehicles—all moving through a grid of constantly changing variables. With traditional systems, traffic management was mostly reactive: respond to congestion, adjust signals manually, hope it improves.

With a digital twin, cities like Shanghai are now modeling live traffic behavior at the citywide level. They ingest real-time sensor data from intersections, street cameras, and connected vehicles. The digital twin maps it all into a single, synchronized view—showing where flow is smooth, where it's slowing, and what's likely to happen next.

From there, it can:

- Adjust traffic signals on the fly
- Reroute vehicles dynamically based on congestion
- Predict surges during events or emergencies
- Simulate policy changes (e.g., new bike lanes or toll pricing) before implementation

It's a shift from reacting to traffic to orchestrating it.

Energy Usage: Efficiency with Eyes Open

Every system consumes energy—whether it's a smart building adjusting HVAC output, a data center regulating heat, or an industrial site powering massive equipment. But energy usage isn't just a number on a bill. It's a live signal that tells you how your operation is behaving, where waste is occurring, and how you can cut costs without cutting performance.

A digital twin gives you real-time visibility into energy use across the entire environment. Not just "how much," but "where," "when," and "why."

- Is a machine running hot during off-hours?
- Are certain zones consistently over-lit or over-cooled?
- Is your renewable energy input aligned with actual demand?
- Can you predict peak usage periods and automate reductions?

Live energy insights help sustainability teams hit targets, facility managers reduce waste, and finance teams lower costs—all while improving comfort and uptime.

And when energy patterns are linked to human movement or machine cycles, the twin can dynamically adjust systems. If no one's in a room, lights dim and HVAC throttles down. If production ramps up, the twin balances power usage across assets. It's real-time optimization made simple.

Connecting the Dots: From Insight to Action

What makes live operational insights so powerful isn't just the data—it's what you can do with it. When a digital twin knows what's happening right now—and has the intelligence to interpret that in context—it becomes a control center for smarter action.

- A factory slows a robot's movement because a worker is nearby
- A retail store unlocks checkout counters based on line length
- A hospital escalates cleaning protocols when traffic surges in a waiting area
- A facility throttles energy-intensive processes during demand spikes to reduce costs

It's not about having more data. It's about having the right data, in the right place, at the right time—so your systems and people can make decisions that are faster, safer, and smarter.

The Big Picture

Live operational insights are where the promise of the digital twin becomes tangible. It's where visibility becomes clarity—and where clarity becomes control. From foot traffic to traffic jams, from kilowatts to workforce motion, every signal becomes a story. And every story can lead to action.

In a world that doesn't wait, having a live view of your operations isn't just helpful. It's essential. Because if you can't see what's happening now, you're already behind. But when your digital twin is watching, learning, and guiding in real time—you're not just keeping up. You're in control.

Case Study: Mevea's Virtual Machine Lifecycle

Few companies embody the full potential of digital twin technology like Mevea. Their approach doesn't just scratch the surface of virtual modeling—it dives deep into the complete lifecycle of a machine, from design to operation, optimization, and beyond. What makes Mevea's case especially compelling is how seamlessly they've integrated physics-based simulation, real-time feedback, and operator training into a single, evolving system. Their digital twins don't just represent machines—they become part of their DNA.

Let's break down how Mevea applies digital twin technology across every phase of a machine's life—and why it matters.

1. Design and Prototyping: Building Before It Exists

The first phase in Mevea's digital twin lifecycle begins before anything physical is built. Using advanced simulation tools, Mevea creates a fully interactive, physics-accurate digital model of a machine. This virtual prototype isn't just a 3D visualization—it behaves exactly as the real machine would under stress, weight, speed, and other environmental conditions.

This allows engineers to test:

- How the machine performs on different terrains
- What happens under high loads or repetitive motion
- How parts interact and where design flaws might surface

And because the simulation incorporates real-world physics, designers can fail fast—testing multiple iterations without wasting material, time, or money on physical prototypes.

This is the foundation of smart engineering: designing with foresight, optimizing before errors occur, and including stakeholders early in the process through interactive models.

2. Deployment and Real-Time Monitoring: Mirroring the Machine

Once the physical machine is built and deployed, Mevea's digital twin continues to operate in parallel. It connects to real-time data streams—sensor inputs, telemetry, environmental variables—and reflects the machine's current state with precision.

This digital shadow allows for:

- Condition monitoring: detecting abnormal behavior or stress
- Predictive maintenance: forecasting wear before it leads to failure
- Performance tracking: comparing real-world behavior to expected baselines
- Remote diagnostics: identifying issues without physical inspections

With the twin connected to the machine throughout its operation, Mevea enables continuous health awareness—meaning problems can be addressed proactively, reducing unplanned downtime and extending the machine's lifespan.

3. Optimization and Operator Training: A Smarter, Safer Lifecycle

Beyond monitoring, Mevea's digital twin becomes a training and optimization platform. Operators can use the same twin to learn how to control the machine, practice tasks in simulation, and build expertise before stepping into the field.

In training mode, the twin:

- Replicates the real controls and behaviors of the machine
- Exposes trainees to both normal and emergency scenarios
- Provides feedback on decisions, timing, and precision
- Reduces the risk of early errors or safety incidents

But the twin doesn't just train people—it also learns from them. Mevea collects insights from operator behavior and system performance, feeding them back into the simulation engine. This allows the twin to improve over time, offering increasingly personalized and effective training programs.

On the optimization side, engineers can run simulated "what-if" scenarios to refine machine settings, improve energy efficiency, or test new software updates—all without touching the physical machine.

4. Decommissioning and Knowledge Transfer: The Twin Lives On

Eventually, even the best machines reach the end of their lifecycle. But Mevea's digital twin doesn't fade away—it becomes a historical archive and knowledge resource. Every movement, update, and performance change throughout the machine's life is stored and time-stamped.

This data can be used to:

- Analyze lifetime performance trends
- Improve the design of the next generation of machines
- Inform decommissioning strategies, recycling plans, or part reuse
- Transfer operational knowledge to teams working on similar systems

In this final stage, the twin transitions from a live asset to a library of insight—ensuring that the value of one machine doesn't end when its hardware does. Instead, it feeds into a cycle of continuous improvement.

The Full Circle: Value at Every Stage

Mevea's approach to digital twins doesn't treat them as a one-time tool or a narrow-use application. Their platform accompanies the machine through its entire lifecycle, delivering value at every stage:

- Before it's built (design validation)
- While it runs (real-time monitoring and optimization)
- As it evolves (operator training and system updates)

- After it's retired (learning and innovation for the future)

This is the full vision of a digital twin realized—not just a visual replica, but an intelligent companion that lives, learns, and leads alongside its physical counterpart.

In doing so, Mevea shows how digital twins aren't just a trend—they're a fundamental shift in how machines are designed, operated, and continuously improved. And as industries seek smarter, safer, and more sustainable operations, this lifecycle model is becoming the new standard—not just for what's possible, but for what's essential.

The lifecycle of a digital twin is a journey—from concept to creation, from reaction to prediction, and eventually, from digital mirror to intelligent partner. It's not a one-time investment, but a continuous evolution—driven by data, refined through learning, and extended through integration. When nurtured properly, a digital twin becomes more than a system—it becomes a force multiplier. It enables smarter decisions today while paving the way for tomorrow's innovations. And for organizations ready to think long-term, that lifecycle isn't just a timeline—it's a roadmap to transformation.

Chapter 8

Digital Twin vs. Reality–Syncing the Two Worlds

A digital twin is only as powerful as its alignment with the real world. No matter how intelligent or detailed the virtual model, if it falls out of sync with the physical system, the value begins to erode—fast. This chapter explores the delicate, high-stakes relationship between the twin and its real-world counterpart. How do you keep the two in constant conversation? What happens when the connection breaks? And what does it take to maintain trust in a system that's always learning and changing? In the race to automate, optimize, and predict, staying synced isn't a luxury—it's a requirement.

Challenges of Keeping Digital Twins Updated

The promise of a digital twin is seductive: a live, intelligent replica of your system, always in step with reality, always ready to inform, predict, and optimize. But behind that seamless surface lies one of the most complex tasks in digital transformation—keeping the digital twin accurately synced with the physical world. It sounds simple in theory. In practice, it's a moving target.

Maintaining a current, accurate, and responsive twin isn't just about gathering data. It's about managing change—constant, unpredictable, sometimes invisible change. And it requires precision, coordination, and vigilance across systems, teams, and time.

Here's where the biggest challenges lie.

1. Sensor Drift and Hardware Failures

The quality of a digital twin depends entirely on the quality of its inputs. When sensors degrade, misalign, or fail altogether, the twin starts to lose touch with the real world. A temperature sensor reading two degrees too high doesn't seem catastrophic—until it triggers a premature shutdown or masks a genuine overheating event.

Over time, even small inaccuracies snowball. Without rigorous calibration and error checking, the twin begins to reflect a version of reality that looks right, but isn't. And when that trust erodes, the twin becomes nothing more than an expensive dashboard.

2. Software Updates and System Changes

Real-world systems evolve. Machines get upgraded. Workflows are reconfigured. Entire facilities may be restructured. But unless those changes are manually reflected in the twin, the model falls out of date.

Let's say a robot arm gets replaced with a newer version that moves slightly differently. Or a conveyor belt's speed is increased. If those changes aren't mapped into the digital twin, all predictions and simulations based on past configurations become irrelevant—or worse, dangerously misleading.

The challenge here isn't just technical—it's procedural. Organizations must embed digital twin maintenance into their operational culture, with clear protocols for updating the model whenever the physical system changes.

3. Integration Complexity

Most digital twins pull data from a variety of sources: sensors, cameras, IoT platforms, ERP systems, legacy machines, and third-party tools. Each one may operate on its own update schedule, data format, and communication protocol.

As a result, maintaining synchronization becomes a constant juggling act. If just one data stream lags behind or becomes inconsistent, it can cause cascading inaccuracies. And if the integration platform isn't built for scale or flexibility, even minor changes—like adding a new device or adjusting a workflow—can break the system.

This complexity grows exponentially as twins scale from single machines to entire factories, cities, or ecosystems.

4. Latency and Bandwidth Constraints

Even in well-integrated systems, delays in data transmission can cause a digital twin to fall seconds—or even minutes—behind real time. For latency-bound twins (like Google Maps), this may be acceptable. But in environments where timing is critical—manufacturing, logistics, energy, healthcare—a few seconds can mean the difference between optimized response and costly delay.

Edge computing helps by processing data locally before sending it to the cloud, but that introduces a new layer of coordination. How do you ensure the cloud-based model and the edge-based actions stay aligned? This balancing act between speed and synchronization is a constant challenge.

5. Human Error and Oversight

As with any system, the weakest link can often be human. If maintenance logs aren't updated, if configuration changes aren't communicated, if manual overrides go undocumented, the digital twin will quickly fall behind.

And because twins are often highly automated, small oversights can lead to large consequences. An outdated calibration file or an incorrect sensor mapping can quietly skew results for days before anyone notices.

Keeping the twin updated means ensuring accountability and discipline, not just at the technical level, but across every team that interacts with the physical system.

6. Security and Data Integrity

In a world where digital twins are fed by real-time, cloud-connected infrastructure, security becomes inseparable from accuracy. If a data stream is compromised—whether through cyberattack or internal error—the twin may reflect corrupted information.

It's not just a security threat. It's a trust threat. If decision-makers can't trust the twin to reflect reality, they stop using it. And once trust is lost, rebuilding it takes more than just fixing the data—it requires re-proving the system's reliability from the ground up.

7. Model Degradation Over Time

Even if data is clean and systems are synced, the model itself can drift. Machine learning algorithms are trained on historical data—but if the system they're modeling evolves, the model may become less accurate over time.

For instance, a predictive maintenance model trained on last year's equipment behavior might miss new failure patterns if components or usage conditions have changed. Without ongoing retraining and validation, the intelligence layer of the twin can become stale—even as the data remains current.

Meeting the Challenge: Sync as a Discipline

Keeping a digital twin updated isn't a one-time project. It's a discipline—a continuous commitment to alignment between the digital and physical. That means:

- Building robust error detection and calibration workflows
- Embedding model updates into change management processes
- Investing in adaptive, standards-based integration platforms

- Regularly auditing data quality and algorithm performance
- Making synchronization a shared responsibility across departments

The goal isn't perfection. It's resilience—a system that can adapt to change, flag discrepancies, and self-correct when things drift. Because in a world that never stops moving, the value of a digital twin lives or dies by its ability to stay in step.

And when that sync is maintained—when the digital model reflects the real world with precision and speed—you unlock a kind of operational clarity most businesses only dream of.

Accuracy, Latency, and Fidelity: The Three Pillars of Trustworthy Digital Twins

For a digital twin to deliver meaningful value, three technical pillars must remain rock solid: accuracy, latency, and fidelity. These aren't just abstract performance metrics—they're the core ingredients that define whether your twin can be trusted, relied on, and used for real-time decision-making. When they're in harmony, a digital twin becomes a living mirror of your system. When one slips, the entire model begins to blur.

Let's break down what each of these pillars means, why they matter, and how they work together to determine the effectiveness of your digital twin.

Accuracy: The Truth in Every Data Point

Accuracy is about how closely the digital twin reflects the current state of its physical counterpart. Are the measurements correct? Are the system states true to reality? When the twin shows a component at 65°C, is that actually what's happening on the machine?

This extends beyond raw sensor values—it includes spatial positions, process steps, user actions, and system status. If a robot arm is two centimeters off in the model, that's not just a detail—it could be the difference between collision avoidance and a catastrophic error.

Achieving high accuracy requires:

- Well-calibrated sensors
- Reliable data inputs with minimal noise
- Consistent data validation and error correction
- Tight synchronization between digital and physical updates

And the challenge grows as systems become more complex. When you're syncing entire buildings, cities, or multi-machine production lines, even small inaccuracies can scale into major blind spots. This is why companies like Mevea and Intel emphasize physics-based simulation and precise spatial mapping—accuracy isn't a feature. It's a foundation.

Latency: The Delay That Changes Everything

Latency is the delay between when something happens in the physical world and when it's reflected in the digital twin. If a part fails or a person enters a restricted zone, how quickly does the twin react?

In some applications—like predictive maintenance or long-term planning—a few seconds or minutes of delay might be acceptable. But in real-time environments like smart factories, autonomous systems, or medical monitoring, even a two-second lag can create risk or inefficiency.

Low latency enables:

- Instantaneous alerts for anomalies
- Real-time control of equipment or environments
- Immediate visualization of changes in spatial awareness
- Accurate simulation of time-sensitive interactions

High latency, on the other hand, creates a gap between perception and reality. Decisions based on delayed data become less effective—or outright dangerous. That's why edge computing is often essential for latency-critical systems, processing data closer to the source and responding faster than cloud-based systems alone.

Verizon's 5G-enabled networks help push latency down to the millisecond range, supporting use cases where every second counts—like traffic rerouting, robotic coordination, and remote control of machinery.

Fidelity: The Depth and Realism of the Model

Fidelity refers to how richly the twin captures the complexity of the real-world system. It's not just about the correctness of values (accuracy), but the detail, resolution, and behavioral nuance of the model.

Think of fidelity as the difference between:

- A basic schematic vs. a fully rendered 3D model
- A surface-level animation vs. a physics-based simulation
- A status flag that says "on/off" vs. a model that simulates torque, pressure, and resistance

High-fidelity twins simulate how things really behave—not just how they appear. They account for physics, wear-and-tear, multiple variables interacting, and unexpected scenarios. This is especially important in sectors like manufacturing, where understanding how machines respond under load or stress can make or break operational efficiency.

But fidelity comes with a cost. More detail means more data, more compute, and more need for bandwidth. That's why fidelity must be purpose-driven—you don't always need to simulate every bolt and bearing. The goal is to model enough reality to make reliable decisions, without overwhelming the system.

How They Work Together: The Sync Triangle

Accuracy, latency, and fidelity don't operate in silos—they're deeply interconnected. Push one too hard, and you may compromise the others.

- High accuracy + low latency + high fidelity = Ideal, but requires robust infrastructure and edge/cloud integration.
- High fidelity + high latency = Beautiful model, but not useful for real-time decisions.
- Low fidelity + high accuracy = Fast and clean, but may miss critical complexity.
- High accuracy + low fidelity = Efficient for monitoring, but poor for simulation or training.

Striking the right balance depends entirely on the use case.

A predictive maintenance twin might prioritize accuracy and fidelity, tolerating some latency.

A safety-critical robotics twin must prioritize low latency and high accuracy, even if that means simplifying the model's fidelity.

Understanding these trade-offs is crucial when designing your twin. The worst-case scenario isn't just a slow or shallow model—it's a convincing but inaccurate one. Because when your twin looks right but isn't aligned with reality, it creates a false sense of confidence—and that's when costly mistakes happen.

Precision You Can Trust

The best digital twins don't aim for perfection—they aim for trustworthy precision. That means:

- Accuracy that reflects what's happening now
- Latency low enough to matter in the moment
- Fidelity deep enough to capture what counts

When these three elements are in sync, your digital twin becomes more than just a mirror. It becomes a strategic tool—one that can forecast, guide, and respond in lockstep with reality. Because in a world moving at real-time speed, clarity isn't just helpful—it's power.

Real-Time Feedback vs. Batched Updates: The Timing That Defines Trust

In the world of digital twins, how and when data flows into the system can mean the difference between insight and irrelevance. This brings us to a fundamental choice that every organization must make when designing its twin infrastructure: real-time feedback or batched updates. Both methods serve a purpose. But they serve very different needs, and understanding the distinction is critical to building a digital twin that aligns with your goals.

At the core, this isn't just a technical debate—it's a strategic decision about timing, trust, and control.

Real-Time Feedback: The Pulse of the System

Real-time feedback means the digital twin receives data continuously, with little to no delay. Sensors, IoT devices, and systems stream information directly into the twin as events occur—second by second, or even millisecond by millisecond. The twin reflects the present moment, offering a live view of operations that is always up to date.

This setup is essential for scenarios where timing is mission-critical:

- A robotic arm detecting a person entering its path
- A conveyor belt adjusting speed to match flow demand
- A smart city rerouting traffic to avoid congestion
- A medical device alerting staff to a sudden change in vitals

With real-time feedback, decisions are made in the now. The twin doesn't just observe—it reacts. It powers automated systems, supports urgent decisions, and prevents problems before they escalate.

Benefits of real-time feedback:

- Instant detection of anomalies, hazards, or inefficiencies
- Closed-loop control where the system can act autonomously
- Seamless user experiences, like dynamic environments or AR/VR overlays
- Higher accuracy in time-sensitive simulations and predictions

But real-time feedback comes with demands:

- Requires low-latency networks (like 5G or edge computing)
- Demands high bandwidth and constant data flow
- Needs robust security to protect real-time streams

- Must be engineered for reliability—gaps or outages can break the system

Real-time systems are more complex and expensive to build. But in environments where decisions depend on live information, they're non-negotiable.

Batched Updates: Periodic, Predictable, and Scalable

Batched updates operate on a different rhythm. Instead of a constant stream, data is collected over time and uploaded or synchronized at regular intervals—every few minutes, hourly, or even daily. The digital twin is updated in chunks, not in real time.

This approach works well for scenarios where instant updates aren't required, and where operations are more about analysis and trend monitoring than live interaction.

- Reviewing production efficiency at the end of a shift
- Monitoring building energy usage every 24 hours
- Tracking supply chain movements in daily snapshots
- Updating digital twins in remote areas with poor connectivity

Benefits of batched updates:

- Lower infrastructure costs, since real-time bandwidth isn't required
- Easier to manage and less sensitive to network reliability
- Suitable for post-event analysis and longer-term planning
- Reduces the volume of noise from constant data chatter

However, batched updates create blind spots. If something critical happens between updates—a mechanical failure, an unsafe condition, or a sudden spike in demand—it won't be seen until the next batch arrives. For some industries, that's a dealbreaker.

The Trade-Off: Speed vs. Scale

Choosing between real-time feedback and batched updates isn't about picking a winner. It's about aligning architecture with need.

- If your operations depend on immediate reaction—you need real-time.
- If your focus is on efficiency, planning, or historical trends—batching is enough.

Most modern digital twins, especially at enterprise scale, adopt a hybrid approach. Critical systems—like safety monitoring, robotic coordination, or patient health—run on real-time feedback. Meanwhile, supporting systems—like billing, compliance, or long-term analytics—operate on batched updates.

This split strategy allows organizations to prioritize their resources while still getting the benefits of digital twin intelligence across the board.

Real-Time vs. Batched: A Side-by-Side Snapshot

Feature	Real-Time Feedback	Batched Updates
Latency	Milliseconds to seconds	Minutes to hours
Best For	Automation, safety, control	Reporting, analysis, planning
Infrastructure Needs	High bandwidth, edge compute, 5G	Standard cloud or on-prem systems
Examples	Traffic management, robotics, AR/VR	ERP updates, maintenance logs
Cost & Complexity	Higher	Lower

Risk of Delay	Very low	Higher, depending on batch timing

Syncing Both Worlds

The key is not just choosing one or the other—it's knowing where each belongs. Digital twins can operate in multi-speed mode: fast where they need to act, slower where they only need to inform.

For example, a manufacturing facility might use real-time feedback to coordinate machines and worker movement, while relying on batched updates for end-of-day performance reporting and quality audits.

When these systems are well-integrated, they reinforce each other. Real-time alerts can trigger batch reports. Batched data can retrain real-time models. And the entire operation benefits from clarity across time scales.

In the end, it's not about speed alone—it's about relevance. A perfectly accurate insight delivered too late is worthless. But a fast insight based on outdated or partial data is dangerous.

A smart digital twin strategy respects both sides of this equation. It knows when to act instantly—and when to wait, reflect, and learn. Because timing isn't just technical. In digital twin systems, timing is everything.

Real-Time Feedback vs. Batched Updates: Timing Is Everything

The power of a digital twin doesn't lie in its visuals or dashboards. It lies in timing. The moment a machine malfunctions, a person walks into a restricted area, or an energy spike hits the system, timing determines whether the twin reacts in sync or just watches it happen too late. That's where the divide between real-time feedback and batched updates becomes critical.

Real-time feedback means the twin is living, breathing—reacting instantly, learning continuously, and guiding decisions in the moment. Batched updates mean it checks in periodically, catching up on what happened after the fact. Both have their place. But they're built for very different kinds of work.

In high-stakes, fast-moving environments—like automated factories, autonomous vehicles, or patient monitoring—real-time feedback is non-negotiable. Latency becomes risk. The system needs to know what's happening now, not what happened ten minutes ago.

With real-time feedback, the digital twin becomes more than an observer—it becomes a co-pilot. Machines adjust their own behavior based on incoming data. Systems course-correct mid-process. Alerts go out before a failure escalates. And humans rely on it because it stays ahead of the curve.

But not every system needs to fire on all cylinders 24/7. In slower-moving environments—like supply chain analysis, building energy reporting, or quarterly maintenance reviews—batched updates are efficient, cost-effective, and perfectly adequate. These twins don't need to act in real time. They need to inform. They show patterns. They support planning. And they do it without the bandwidth and infrastructure demands that come with a constant live feed.

The smartest systems do both. They use real-time feedback where timing matters most, and batched updates where insight matters more than immediacy. And when the two sync together, businesses get the best of both worlds—instant awareness where it counts, and deep analysis where it drives the future.

In digital twin architecture, timing isn't just a technical decision. It's a strategic one. Because the value of any insight isn't just in knowing—it's in knowing before it's too late to act.

From Autonomous Driving to Jarvis: The Rise of Spatial Understanding

One of the most compelling demonstrations of digital twin technology is happening right now on the road. Autonomous vehicles rely on a kind of real-time digital twin that continuously mirrors their surroundings—mapping not just static roads and landmarks, but dynamic, ever-changing inputs: pedestrians, weather, other vehicles, road signs, even potholes. But it's not just about sensing objects. It's about understanding space.

For an autonomous system to be truly safe and reliable, it has to answer three fundamental questions at all times: What is it? Where is it? When is it happening? This is the same triad Intel's Scenescape platform is built on—combining sensor data, spatial mapping, and precise pose detection to give machines spatial intelligence that mirrors human intuition.

Think of a self-driving car approaching a busy intersection. It sees a person at the curb, a cyclist moving between lanes, a delivery van partially blocking a stop sign. Without understanding where those objects are in 3D space—how fast they're moving, what their likely path is, and how they relate to one another—the car can't make a safe decision. A camera alone isn't enough. The system needs context—a constantly updating model of its surroundings.

That's a real-time spatial twin in action. But this technology isn't limited to vehicles. The same principles are being applied in factories, smart buildings, retail stores, hospitals—even cities.

Intelligent Scenes: Environments That Think

Now imagine environments that not only reflect the world in real time but respond to it—buildings that know who's inside, where they're moving, and how to optimize everything from lighting to safety protocols. That's where digital twins are headed: intelligent scenes that interpret, adapt, and even collaborate with the people and machines within them.

In a smart warehouse, for example, the digital twin tracks every AGV (automated guided vehicle), every worker, and every moving pallet. When someone enters a blind corner, the system slows nearby robots, adjusts lighting, and alerts nearby machinery to prevent collisions. It's not just monitoring movement—it's predicting outcomes and coordinating responses, moment to moment.

This level of spatial intelligence requires not only precise pose detection and calibrated sensors but also a shared coordinate system—so every camera, lidar, robot, and AI algorithm is speaking the same spatial language. When the environment understands itself, it becomes proactive rather than reactive.

Jarvis-Style Systems: The Future of Context-Aware Environments

The next leap is systems that don't just respond—they interact.

Picture a control center like Iron Man's Jarvis—but instead of a sci-fi fantasy, it's your actual office, factory, or campus. You walk in, and the system knows your location, preferences, and role. It brings up the latest performance data as you approach your workstation. It alerts you if a critical part is nearing failure. It suggests schedule changes based on foot traffic patterns and inventory flow. Lights follow you, air conditioning adapts to movement, and safety systems activate preemptively.

These context-aware environments aren't far off. They're being prototyped today using the same technologies that power advanced digital twins—scene graphs, real-time spatial mapping, multimodal tracking, and machine learning layered over 3D space.

As these systems evolve, they'll shift from tools we use to partners we work with. Not just data-driven, but context-driven. Not just reactive, but anticipatory.

Digital twins began as a way to simulate machines. But in their most advanced form, they evolve into spatial intelligence engines—capable of understanding the world as it unfolds, predicting what comes next, and adapting the environment accordingly. From autonomous vehicles navigating chaos to buildings that think, guide, and respond, we're moving toward a future where the twin is more than a mirror.

It becomes the brain behind the world we live in.

The magic of a digital twin lies in its ability to mirror reality—but the impact comes when that mirror is precise, live, and responsive. Syncing the two worlds—digital and physical—is what transforms data into insight, models into decisions, and technology into trust. It's not about perfection—it's about alignment. Because when your twin and your world move in step, you're no longer just observing operations—you're shaping them, moment by moment. And in that space, where real and virtual meet, the future of business is being built.

PART III

APPLYING DIGITAL TWINS ACROSS INDUSTRIES

Chapter 9

Manufacturing and Industrial Systems

If there's one industry where digital twins have already proven their worth, it's manufacturing. In a space where milliseconds matter, margins are tight, and every breakdown carries real cost, the ability to simulate, monitor, and optimize physical systems in real time isn't just helpful—it's transformational. Digital twins are redefining how products are designed, how factories are run, and how machines are maintained. This chapter dives into the core of industrial application—where digital meets mechanical, and where precision pays off.

Simulating Machines Before Production: Building It Right Before It's Built at All

In traditional manufacturing, the first prototype often comes with a cost: delays, rework, unexpected design flaws, and materials wasted on trial and error. It's a phase where issues get uncovered late—when they're most expensive to fix. But with digital twin technology, that reality is being rewritten. Today, manufacturers can simulate machines in full fidelity before a single bolt is tightened, allowing them to test, iterate, and perfect designs virtually—long before physical production begins.

This isn't just about 3D modeling. It's about physics-based, data-driven simulation that mirrors how a machine will behave in the real world. It takes into account load, resistance, environmental conditions, friction, torque, movement—all the nuances that separate theoretical design from actual performance.

Virtual Prototypes with Real-World Precision

Companies like Mevea are leading this shift. Their digital twin platform allows manufacturers to build a fully functional, virtual version of a machine—complete with control systems, hydraulic behavior, and mechanical interactions. Engineers can simulate how it moves on different terrain, how it responds under pressure, and how various components interact under real-world stress.

This lets teams:

- Validate mechanical design early in the process

- Optimize component layout for performance and longevity
- Identify critical failure points or design weaknesses
- Run stress tests without putting any hardware at risk

All of this happens before a physical unit ever leaves the CAD environment. That's massive. It shortens development cycles, reduces costs, and eliminates surprises at the worst possible stage—production.

Faster Iterations, Better Products

Because simulations are virtual, design teams can test dozens—or hundreds—of design variations in days instead of weeks. They can run "what-if" scenarios: What happens if we increase the payload? How will this gearset perform over 10,000 cycles? Is the current motor spec enough for full-speed operation on a slope?

This turns R&D from a linear, expensive slog into a rapid, dynamic cycle of test, learn, improve. It doesn't just lead to faster production. It leads to smarter products—better tuned to real-world use, more durable, and easier to maintain.

And by simulating the entire machine lifecycle, including wear and maintenance behavior, engineers can build with the long game in mind—not just designing for function, but for uptime, serviceability, and longevity.

Involving Stakeholders Early

Another powerful advantage of pre-production simulation is that it invites collaboration across teams. Stakeholders can interact with the digital twin during the design phase—reviewing ergonomics, visualizing access points, verifying controls, and even participating in virtual walkthroughs.

This de-risks the design process by giving early visibility to those who'll be responsible for operation, safety, training, and maintenance. Issues that used to surface only after production can now be caught during simulation.

From Virtual Testing to Operator Training

What's more, that same simulated machine can be used to train operators before the real thing is ever delivered. By the time the first physical unit arrives, teams are already fluent in its controls, behavior, and quirks—minimizing ramp-up time and early misuse.

This closes the loop between design and deployment in a way that was previously impossible. The machine's digital twin becomes a bridge—not just between engineering and production, but between R&D and the people who will actually use the equipment in the field.

Designing for Reality, Not Just Specs

The value of simulating machines before production isn't just about speed or savings. It's about clarity. About designing with full understanding of how a product will live, work, and wear over time. It means fewer assumptions, fewer last-minute surprises, and far less waste—both in materials and in time.

In manufacturing, where every error compounds, and every hour of downtime counts, building right the first time is everything. Digital twins make that possible—not with more guesswork, but with better foresight. Not with more effort, but with smarter design. And in that shift, the rules of production are changing for good.

Predictive Maintenance and Reduced Downtime

& Safety and Automation Integration

In the high-stakes world of industrial manufacturing, downtime is the silent killer. A single unplanned stop can ripple across production lines, delay deliveries, inflate costs, and hit customer confidence. Traditionally, maintenance was either reactive (fix it when it breaks) or scheduled (fix it whether it needs it or not). Both approaches lead to waste—either in emergency response or in unnecessary intervention. But digital twins bring a third way: predictive maintenance powered by real-time data, historical patterns, and intelligent forecasting.

This isn't theory. It's happening now.

Predictive Maintenance: See It Coming, Before It Comes

A digital twin constantly monitors machine health—not just performance at the surface level, but the early, often invisible signs of wear and strain that precede failure. Through integrated sensors and AI models, the twin learns what "normal" looks like and flags when the system begins to drift from baseline. Slight increases in vibration, heat, pressure variation, or cycle time deviations become warning signs.

Instead of waiting for a breakdown or blindly swapping out parts, predictive maintenance enables:

- Timely intervention: Fix what's failing, not what's functioning.
- Reduced spare parts inventory: No more overstocking "just in case."
- Fewer surprises: Maintenance becomes a scheduled, strategic event—not a crisis.
- Lower labor costs: Technicians address issues with purpose, not guesswork.

- Extended asset lifespan: Equipment isn't overworked to failure or prematurely retired.

Intel's work with Scenescape showcases this beautifully. When combined with spatial mapping and pose detection, a digital twin doesn't just say something is wrong—it shows where the issue is, what it's affecting, and when it's likely to escalate. This location-aware intelligence eliminates ambiguity and allows for precision targeting.

Beyond Maintenance: Eliminating Downtime Altogether

In more advanced systems, the digital twin doesn't just flag failure—it avoids it completely. By analyzing patterns across machines, shifts, and environments, the twin can simulate the impact of future conditions. For example:

- Will increased throughput next quarter overstress this motor?
- Will humidity during summer months reduce tolerances in this process?
- Will running this cycle overnight create thermal buildup that leads to breakdown?

The twin models those scenarios ahead of time, offering proactive strategies. It can even recommend process changes—adjusting speeds, routes, or loads automatically to balance efficiency with longevity. That's when the twin stops being a monitoring tool and becomes a true advisor.

Safety and Automation Integration: A Unified Intelligence

Downtime isn't the only risk on the floor. Human safety remains a constant priority—and digital twins are now playing a central role in making workplaces safer by design.

When safety systems operate in silos—separate from automation, machine controls, and monitoring—they can miss critical cues. A robot might move blindly through a space where a worker just entered. A process might restart after shutdown without confirming that the zone is clear. A maintenance door might open while machinery is still live.

With a digital twin that integrates safety and automation, all of these systems communicate in real time. Cameras, sensors, badge readers, control logic, and emergency protocols are synchronized through a shared spatial and temporal model. This allows the twin to:

- Detect when a person enters a restricted area and halt nearby machinery instantly

- Monitor whether PPE is being worn in hazardous zones
- Prevent machines from restarting if someone is still within danger range
- Alert supervisors to repeated near-miss behaviors or compliance violations
- Simulate evacuation or lockdown scenarios under different threat conditions

It's not just about reaction. It's about situational awareness—the kind humans take for granted, but machines have historically lacked. With digital twins, that gap is closing.

The Power of Coordination

Predictive maintenance and safety often happen in parallel—but when they're linked through a digital twin, the results multiply.

Imagine a scenario where a piece of equipment is showing signs of failure. The twin not only schedules service—it adjusts workflows around the machine, reroutes tasks to other lines, and ensures that nearby systems account for potential hazards during the repair. Workers are warned in advance. Technicians are guided precisely. Downtime is minimized, and risk is eliminated.

All of this is possible because the twin sees the full picture—people, machines, systems, and space—coordinated through a unified digital environment.

Smarter Systems. Safer People.

Digital twins don't just make factories more efficient. They make them more human-aware. By anticipating failure, guiding response, and coordinating action across safety and automation systems, they elevate the workplace into something smarter, calmer, and more resilient.

In a world where seconds matter and safety is non-negotiable, these capabilities aren't just upgrades. They're necessities. And for manufacturers who get this right, the return isn't just in saved time or money—it's in lives protected, chaos avoided, and systems that don't just work, but work together.

Factory-Wide Visibility and Optimization

& Digital Twins vs. Traditional SCADA

In many manufacturing environments, visibility has long been a patchwork—isolated systems, siloed departments, machines monitored in fragments rather than as part of a unified whole. Traditional approaches like SCADA

(Supervisory Control and Data Acquisition) have been the go-to for years, giving operators a basic look into machine states, alarms, and process conditions. But those systems weren't built for today's complexity. They weren't designed to scale across entire facilities, integrate spatial data, or provide predictive insights. That's where digital twins redefine the playing field—not as a replacement for SCADA, but as a new layer of intelligence.

Factory-Wide Visibility: One System, One Source of Truth

Imagine being able to view your entire plant floor—every machine, every worker, every flow of material—on a live, spatially accurate map. Not a dashboard with numbers and status lights, but a 3D environment that mirrors reality in real time. That's the power of a factory-scale digital twin.

With a digital twin:

- You don't just see that a machine is overheating—you see where it's located, what other systems it's connected to, and whether anyone is nearby.
- You don't just know that production slowed down—you trace the issue back to a delayed material delivery or a misrouted pallet.

- You don't just monitor cycle times—you analyze patterns over time, correlate them with operator shifts, temperature changes, or upstream issues.

This kind of visibility makes root cause analysis faster, leaner operations possible, and informed, system-wide decisions the norm. It connects what used to be disconnected: people, processes, machines, and space.

In effect, the entire factory becomes legible—not just to engineers, but to leadership, planning teams, and even AI systems trained to detect inefficiencies.

Optimization Through Live Insight and Simulation

Once you have that full-picture visibility, optimization becomes continuous. You're not reacting to yesterday's problems—you're adjusting to today's conditions and modeling tomorrow's improvements.

A digital twin can:

- Reroute processes when a line slows or stops
- Balance workloads across multiple production cells
- Recommend staffing changes based on foot traffic and task complexity
- Simulate new workflows before implementing them on the floor

- Monitor KPIs across departments in context—not just by the numbers, but by behavior

And unlike static systems, the twin learns. It refines its predictions based on live outcomes, creating a loop of constant improvement that traditional monitoring tools simply can't match.

Digital Twins vs. Traditional SCADA: What's the Difference?

SCADA systems have been manufacturing's operational backbone for decades. They collect data from sensors and PLCs, send alerts, provide HMIs (Human-Machine Interfaces), and control processes remotely. But they're narrow in scope—built to monitor equipment, not understand it. They're great at telling you what just happened, but not why it happened, how it might affect the broader system, or how to prevent it next time.

Here's how digital twins break out of that mold:

Feature	SCADA	Digital Twin
Scope	Equipment-focused	System-wide, spatial, contextual

Data Type	Real-time signals, alarms	Real-time + historical + spatial + predictive
Visualization	2D dashboards, status panels	3D interactive environments
Predictive Capabilities	Minimal	Built-in AI/ML forecasting
Simulation	Not supported	Core function (test before deploy)
Integration	Typically siloed	Multi-system, multimodal integration
Learning	Static logic	Adaptive and self-improving

The key difference isn't just in features—it's in philosophy. SCADA reacts. Digital twins anticipate. SCADA shows machine states. Digital twins show machine behavior in context. And most importantly, SCADA is a tool for monitoring, while digital twins are platforms for decision-making.

That doesn't mean SCADA is obsolete. In fact, many digital twin systems integrate with SCADA to ingest its data as one layer among many. But the twin takes that data further—combining it with spatial tracking, machine learning, and cross-system logic to elevate awareness and action across the entire factory.

One Factory. One Model. Infinite Leverage.

In the digital twin–enabled factory, you don't need a dozen dashboards and guesswork to manage operations. You have a unified environment where you can see it all, understand it fast, and change it intelligently.

And while SCADA gave us the ability to monitor processes, digital twins are giving us something bigger: the ability to model outcomes, optimize continuously, and operate with precision at scale.

This is how factories are becoming smarter—not by replacing every legacy system overnight, but by layering intelligence on top of them. By turning fragmented visibility into a connected model. And by moving from reactive control to proactive command.

Intel's Scenescape and Mevea: Real-World Case Examples of Digital Twins in Action

Talk is cheap without proof—and digital twins are no longer just buzzwords or theoretical frameworks. Companies like Intel and Mevea are leading by example, building and deploying real digital twin solutions that solve real operational challenges in real environments. These aren't one-off projects—they're evolving platforms built to scale, adapt, and deliver measurable value. Let's explore how each one brings the digital twin concept to life in distinct, powerful ways.

Intel's Scenescape: Real-Time Spatial Intelligence for Safer, Smarter Environments

Intel's Scenescape is more than just a monitoring tool—it's a spatial awareness platform designed to bring real-time intelligence to physical spaces. Think of it as a live, 3D map of your environment, constantly updated by cameras, sensors, and AI, capable of tracking what's happening, where it's happening, and when it happens—down to the millisecond.

Use Case: Factory Floor Spatial Coordination

In industrial settings, Scenescape creates a digital twin of the entire production environment, including machines, people, and pathways. Cameras and sensors feed into the system, which uses pose detection and calibrated spatial data to understand the exact position and movement of every object.

Let's say a forklift is moving through a corridor while an AGV is headed toward a blind corner. Traditional systems might not connect the dots in time. Scenescape does. It knows the location and trajectory of both objects, calculates collision risk in real time, and automatically slows the AGV or triggers an alert—preventing accidents before they happen.

Key benefits delivered by Scenescape:

- Multimodal sensor fusion: Combines video, lidar, and other inputs into one coherent spatial model.
- Predictive movement tracking: Learns and anticipates movement patterns to forecast outcomes.
- Environmental mapping: Maintains an always-current 3D representation of complex environments.
- Plug-and-play interoperability: Integrates with existing security, automation, and safety systems.

Beyond factories, Scenescape has been applied in retail, healthcare, and urban infrastructure, where real-time spatial awareness enhances safety, efficiency, and user experience. From catching intruders to guiding autonomous robots, Scenescape is a clear example of how digital twins move beyond data—they provide situational understanding.

Mevea: Physics-Based Simulation from Design to Operation

Where Scenescape focuses on live environments, Mevea shines in the engineering and lifecycle simulation domain. Mevea's digital twins are built with physics-level accuracy, enabling manufacturers to simulate machines in virtual space before they're ever produced—and to continue learning from them once they are.

Use Case: Heavy Machinery Prototyping and Operator Training

Using Mevea, manufacturers create virtual versions of heavy-duty equipment—like excavators, cranes, or agricultural machines—that mimic not only their appearance but also their real-world physical behavior. These virtual machines can be driven, operated, and tested in different terrains and conditions—right down to hydraulic behavior, load response, and control logic.

Engineers can simulate extreme conditions, mechanical stress, operator error, and failure scenarios, all before committing to physical prototyping. Once the machine is in the field, the same digital twin can be used for operator training and performance monitoring.

Mevea's advantages in practice:

- Reduced need for physical prototypes: Saving time, money, and material waste.
- Improved design validation: Discover and resolve issues early in the development process.
- Simulation-based operator training: Hands-on experience in a safe, repeatable environment.
- Lifecycle integration: The digital twin evolves with the machine—learning from live data, informing upgrades.

Because Mevea models the entire machine lifecycle, it's not just a design tool—it becomes part of the long-term strategy for quality, safety, and performance. And by simulating everything from joint fatigue to operator workflows, it helps build smarter products and smarter people.

Two Perspectives, One Vision

Together, Scenescape and Mevea offer a compelling full-spectrum view of what digital twins can do:

- Mevea handles the front end—design, simulation, training, and optimization.
- Scenescape takes over during live deployment—tracking, reacting, and adapting in real time.

Both platforms demonstrate that digital twins aren't confined to one part of the product lifecycle. They can support everything, from R&D to operations, maintenance, and safety—across environments, industries, and use cases.

And most importantly, these are not future concepts. They're operational, scalable, and delivering value today.

For companies considering the jump into digital twin technology, these platforms offer a clear message: this isn't experimental anymore. It's real. It works. And the sooner you implement it, the sooner your systems stop reacting—and start thinking.

Manufacturing isn't what it used to be—and it can't afford to be. Digital twins give industrial operations the edge they need to stay agile, reduce waste, and prevent failure before it happens. From early-stage prototyping to predictive maintenance and adaptive workflows, the factory of the future is no longer a place of guesswork—it's a responsive, intelligent ecosystem. In this space, digital twins are no longer optional. They're essential.

Chapter 10

Smart Cities and Infrastructure

Cities are no longer just collections of buildings, roads, and utilities—they're evolving into intelligent ecosystems powered by data, connectivity, and digital context. As urban centers face growing pressure to be safer, cleaner, more efficient, and more responsive, digital twins are emerging as the core infrastructure behind the transformation. This chapter explores how cities around the world are turning physical space into digital environments—where traffic flows can be optimized in real time, energy grids can self-balance, and services can adapt to human behavior dynamically.

Shanghai's Digital Twin Model: A City That Sees Itself

Shanghai isn't just one of the world's most populous cities—it's also one of the most digitally advanced. With more than 24 million residents, sprawling infrastructure, and a complex blend of commercial, industrial, and residential zones, Shanghai presents a massive coordination challenge. But instead of relying solely on traditional urban planning and fragmented control systems, the city has built something far more ambitious: a city-scale digital twin.

This isn't a buzzword implementation or a limited pilot. Shanghai has created a live, data-driven replica of its entire metropolitan environment—roads, buildings, utilities, traffic, emergency systems, waste management, and more—all connected, visualized, and operated through a central digital platform. It's one of the most sophisticated examples of urban digital twinning anywhere in the world.

A Real-Time Virtual City

The goal of Shanghai's digital twin is simple: see everything, understand it, and act on it. This means having full situational awareness of what's happening across the city at any given moment. It pulls live data from thousands of sources—traffic cameras, public transportation systems, IoT sensors in buildings, air quality monitors, power grids, and citizen feedback systems.

But what sets it apart is that it doesn't just collect data—it maps it spatially, in real time. Officials and city planners can explore the digital twin in a 3D environment, zooming into specific districts, buildings, or intersections to view conditions as they unfold. If there's a traffic jam, they can see not just the congestion but the ripple effects. If there's a public safety incident, emergency responders can be dispatched faster, with contextual knowledge of the space and people involved.

The city essentially has a virtual command center, where decision-makers interact with the entire urban landscape as if they're inside it.

Use Cases That Drive Real Results

Shanghai's digital twin isn't a futuristic concept—it's already delivering tangible outcomes:

- Traffic Flow Optimization: The system monitors real-time vehicle movement across thousands of intersections and roads. Algorithms adjust traffic signals dynamically, reroute vehicles, and reduce congestion based on live demand.

- Waste Management: Sensors embedded in collection systems report fill levels and pickup patterns. The digital twin models optimal routes for sanitation vehicles, reducing fuel usage and improving coverage.

- Environmental Monitoring: The platform tracks air pollution, noise levels, and temperature across city zones. Alerts are triggered for unhealthy spikes, and mitigation efforts can be coordinated faster.

- Public Safety and Emergency Response: In the event of a disaster or major incident, the city can simulate various scenarios, model escape routes, and guide responders with spatially accurate overlays.

- Urban Planning: Before new construction or zoning changes happen, planners test the impact in the digital twin. How will a new skyscraper affect traffic? Will a new park change foot traffic patterns? It's all tested virtually before breaking ground.

A Living, Learning Infrastructure

What makes Shanghai's digital twin remarkable is its continuous evolution. It's not a static model—it's a learning system that adapts over time. With every new data stream, every public input, and every urban change, the twin gets smarter. AI and machine learning refine its predictions, helping the city not just respond to problems—but anticipate them.

And the city's investment doesn't stop at monitoring. Shanghai is exploring ways to simulate policy impacts in advance—testing economic reforms, energy policies, and sustainability initiatives inside the digital twin before rolling them out. This turns city management into something more like strategy gaming—where leaders play out outcomes before making real-world moves.

The Blueprint for Future Cities

Shanghai's digital twin is more than a tech showcase—it's a working model of the future of urban governance. It proves that cities can be more than reactive bureaucracies. They can be responsive, dynamic systems—continuously optimizing for the needs of their people.

Other cities—Barcelona, Singapore, Dubai—are taking notes and building their own versions, but Shanghai remains the benchmark. It shows that with the right integration of sensors, data, AI, and spatial modeling, an entire city can think, adapt, and improve in real time.

And in an age of growing urban populations, environmental pressure, and infrastructure strain, that kind of intelligence isn't just impressive—it's essential.

Waste, Traffic, Utility Management

& Urban Planning and Citizen Experience

The complexity of managing a modern city goes far beyond potholes and zoning maps. City leaders today are under pressure to balance sustainability, efficiency, and livability—all while supporting growing populations and aging infrastructure. Digital twins offer a new layer of control, turning every street, system, and structure into a data-driven asset that can be monitored, optimized, and adapted in real time.

And nowhere is this more evident than in four core pillars of urban life: waste, traffic, utility management, and the citizen experience. These aren't isolated departments—they're interconnected systems that affect how people move, live, and work. With a digital twin, cities don't just manage them better—they rethink how they function together.

Waste Management: Smarter, Cleaner Streets

Trash collection might not seem high-tech, but for a city, it's a massive logistical operation. Missed pickups, inefficient routes, and overflowing bins aren't just nuisances—they're public health concerns and quality-of-life issues.

With a digital twin:

- Smart sensors in bins report fill levels in real time
- Routes are dynamically optimized based on need, not a static schedule
- The system models fleet behavior to reduce fuel usage and emissions
- Sanitation crews receive live updates for high-traffic zones or special events
- Long-term waste patterns are analyzed to inform infrastructure investment

What was once a blind, reactive process becomes a proactive, adaptive system that scales with the city's needs.

Traffic Flow: From Congestion to Coordination

Traffic is one of the most visible—and frustrating—symptoms of poor urban coordination. But digital twins transform traffic from a guessing game into a real-time orchestration challenge.

By integrating data from traffic lights, road sensors, GPS-equipped vehicles, public transit, and even pedestrian movement, a digital twin helps cities:

- Adjust signal timing based on live conditions, not fixed intervals

- Reroute traffic in response to accidents, construction, or weather
- Prioritize emergency vehicles and public transport in congested corridors
- Simulate the impact of proposed changes before making them permanent
- Detect traffic build-up before it causes delays

It's not just about moving cars faster. It's about moving everyone smarter—whether they're walking, biking, driving, or riding public transit.

Utility Management: Balancing Demand and Sustainability

Water, electricity, heating, cooling—these aren't just background services. They're critical lifelines, and managing them intelligently is central to both resilience and sustainability.

A city-wide digital twin integrates utility data at scale, allowing operators to:

- Monitor real-time usage patterns across neighborhoods and buildings
- Predict demand surges (like heatwaves or event days) and adjust supply preemptively
- Detect anomalies such as leaks, energy spikes, or equipment failures early

- Coordinate across departments—for instance, aligning construction schedules with maintenance windows
- Support renewable integration, by optimizing when and where solar or wind power feeds into the grid

Over time, the system learns, predicts, and helps cities do more with less, reducing waste while keeping essential services running smoothly.

Urban Planning: Test Before You Build

One of the most powerful features of a digital twin is its ability to simulate the future. Before a shovel hits the ground, cities can test the consequences of every major decision.

Want to build a new high-rise? Use the twin to simulate:

- Shadow impact on surrounding buildings
- Changes in foot and vehicle traffic
- Strain on water, power, and internet infrastructure
- Emergency access and evacuation paths
- Effects on noise, air quality, and pedestrian behavior

These insights let planners engage stakeholders early, anticipate unintended consequences, and ensure development aligns with long-term strategy. It shifts planning from paperwork to interactive decision-making, backed by real data.

The Citizen Experience: Designing for Humans

Perhaps the most underrated benefit of digital twins is how they impact the day-to-day experience of citizens. When systems are coordinated and responsive, people feel the difference—shorter commutes, cleaner streets, safer public spaces, more reliable services.

Digital twins can be used to:

- Monitor crowd density during events for public safety
- Optimize lighting and security in high-traffic pedestrian areas
- Adjust building temperatures and lighting based on occupancy
- Inform citizens of service changes or delays in real time
- Personalize city services based on behavioral patterns

When cities know what's happening, they can respond with empathy and intelligence. It's not about controlling space—it's about collaborating with it, designing cities that adapt to how people actually live, not just how they're supposed to.

In these domains—waste, traffic, utilities, planning, and citizen interaction—digital twins aren't just helping cities operate. They're helping them evolve. Turning public services from rigid systems into responsive networks.

Turning planning from guesswork into simulation. And turning cities into environments that don't just function—but understand.

Smart cities aren't built from scratch—they're shaped by systems that learn, respond, and adapt in real time. Digital twins make that possible. By mirroring urban environments with precision and intelligence, cities gain the visibility and foresight they need to solve today's challenges and plan for tomorrow's demands. Whether it's traffic management, sustainability, emergency response, or urban planning, digital twins are turning cities into living systems—ones that don't just function, but actively think.

Chapter 11

Retail, Logistics, and Autonomous Systems

In industries like retail and logistics, every second counts—and every misstep ripples downstream. These are environments where speed, precision, and coordination are everything. Enter digital twins: not as background analytics tools, but as front-line engines of visibility, prediction, and control. Whether it's tracking the flow of inventory through a warehouse, guiding autonomous delivery systems, or optimizing in-store customer experiences, digital twins are helping businesses move smarter, react faster, and anticipate what's next. This chapter explores how the digital and physical worlds come together in some of the most demanding, fast-moving sectors of the economy.

Amazon Go, Inventory Tracking, and Spatial Awareness: Retail Reimagined in Real Time

Amazon Go isn't just a convenience store—it's a case study in what happens when retail is powered by real-time spatial intelligence. No checkout lines. No barcode scanning. Just walk in, grab what you need, and walk out. Behind that seamless experience is a sophisticated digital twin ecosystem—a layered integration of computer vision, IoT sensors, machine learning, and spatial mapping working together to track everything that moves, without a single manual input.

It's not just revolutionary—it's a glimpse into the future of inventory tracking and customer experience.

Just Walk Out, Powered by the Digital Twin

At the core of Amazon Go's system is the concept of real-time spatial awareness. Hundreds of ceiling-mounted cameras and shelf sensors monitor every product, every hand movement, and every footstep. The system knows who picked up what, when they moved it, if they put it back, and whether they left the store with it. All of this is mapped into a digital environment that mirrors the physical space with astonishing precision.

But this isn't just surveillance. It's automated context-building. The system identifies:

- Which items are removed or returned

- How long a shopper lingers in a certain aisle
- What paths are most commonly taken
- When shelves are nearing depletion
- Where restocking will soon be required

Instead of depending on point-of-sale data or periodic stock counts, the store runs on continuous, invisible inventory tracking—item-level awareness without employee intervention.

Inventory as a Live Data Layer

Traditional retail relies on human inputs—scanning barcodes, logging shipments, and manually checking stock. That introduces lag and error. A digital twin flips the model by making inventory a living data layer, constantly updated and visualized in real time.

- When a product is picked up, inventory adjusts.
- When a delivery arrives, the system knows instantly what's in the shipment and what shelf it belongs to.
- When a high-demand item runs low, predictive models initiate restocking before shelves go empty.

This leads to tighter supply chain coordination, reduced shrinkage, better demand forecasting, and a smoother shopping experience.

In logistics, this kind of tracking extends to entire fulfillment centers. Digital twins model package flow, shelf organization, picker routes, and robotic movement, creating a synchronized view of warehouse operations. Delays are flagged instantly. Bottlenecks are addressed in real time. Efficiency improves by the minute.

Spatial Awareness: Beyond Inventory

What makes Amazon Go's system especially powerful is that it doesn't just track products—it tracks people in space, with the same level of detail. This spatial awareness unlocks deep insights:

- Which store layouts drive higher engagement?
- Where do customers hesitate, backtrack, or abandon items?
- What's the optimal distance between shelves to prevent congestion?
- Can lighting, temperature, or music dynamically adjust based on shopper flow?

All of this turns the store from a static layout into a responsive environment. Not in theory. In practice.

And because the system learns continuously, every visit makes it smarter. It's not just collecting data—it's adapting the experience. That's digital twin thinking applied to retail: a 360° model of space, behavior, and product that evolves in real time.

The Broader Impact: A Retail Twin That Thinks

Amazon Go is leading the charge, but it's only the beginning. Retailers of all sizes are exploring how digital twins can:

- Replace manual cycle counts with automated inventory tracking
- Simulate store redesigns virtually before making physical changes
- Analyze in-store customer behavior the way e-commerce tracks clicks and scrolls
- Train new staff in virtual replicas of actual store layouts
- Balance foot traffic, staffing, and merchandising for real-time efficiency

This shift doesn't just improve operations—it redefines what a store is. It becomes an intelligent, reactive space—designed for flow, stocked with precision, and powered by data that tells a live story of what's working and what's not.

In the world of Amazon Go, shelves are smart, cameras are context-aware, and transactions happen without friction. But beneath all of that magic is the discipline of a digital twin—tracking, learning, predicting, and orchestrating. It's not about replacing people. It's about removing friction, reducing error, and unlocking a new era of intelligent commerce. One where space itself becomes part of the experience. And where real-time awareness isn't just a technical advantage—it's the future of retail.

Warehouse Robotics and Multi-Sensor Tracking: Orchestrating Movement with Precision

Modern warehouses are fast-paced ecosystems where timing, accuracy, and coordination define success. With demand for faster delivery, leaner inventory, and 24/7 operations, traditional human-centric workflows are struggling to keep up. Enter digital twins, paired with robotics and multi-sensor tracking—a combination that's transforming warehouses into intelligent, self-optimizing environments where machines and humans move in harmony, guided by a shared digital brain.

This isn't just automation—it's orchestration.

The Digital Twin as Warehouse Conductor

At the center of the modern smart warehouse is a digital twin that sees everything—robots, shelving units, inventory bins, people, paths, and pallets. The twin tracks all these moving parts in real time, enabling it to:

- Route autonomous mobile robots (AMRs) dynamically based on floor conditions
- Assign tasks to machines and human pickers based on location, speed, and availability
- Predict potential congestion or safety risks before they occur
- Prioritize shipments and loading schedules based on live demand or truck arrivals
- Simulate new workflows or warehouse layouts before implementation

What makes this possible is multi-sensor tracking—an integrated system of cameras, lidar, RFID, IMUs (inertial measurement units), and environmental sensors all feeding data into the digital twin.

Every sensor plays a role:

- Cameras track item movement and shelf activity
- Lidar maps space and obstacle proximity with precision
- RFID tags help locate goods down to the bin level
- IMUs monitor robot acceleration, balance, and movement
- Environmental sensors provide temperature, humidity, and air quality data—crucial for sensitive goods

The twin fuses all of this into a live, spatially aware model that updates continuously, enabling split-second decision-making across thousands of square feet.

From Chaos to Coordination: Robotics in Action

Without coordination, adding robots to a warehouse is like putting race cars on a crowded street—it may be faster, but it's riskier and harder to manage. Digital twins make robotics context-aware.

For example:

- If a human worker steps into a high-traffic zone, the system slows or reroutes nearby AMRs
- If a pallet is misplaced, the twin identifies the anomaly and sends a retrieval command
- If multiple robots need access to the same aisle, the twin sequences their movement to avoid gridlock
- When new inventory arrives, robots are assigned optimal paths for storage based on current warehouse layout and demand forecasts

This turns raw automation into intelligent logistics, where every machine's behavior is optimized in real time—not by a fixed program, but by an adaptive system that understands the environment.

Multi-Robot Collaboration: Like a Factory-Scale Dance

In advanced setups, dozens or even hundreds of robots work together, with each unit acting as both an individual and part of a larger system. The digital twin enables swarm coordination, ensuring:

- No duplication of effort
- Load balancing between robots based on remaining battery life or task load
- Collision avoidance with other robots, humans, and moving inventory
- Coordinated pick-pack-ship sequences to meet tight dispatch windows

This level of coordination requires millisecond-level awareness, something traditional WMS (Warehouse Management Systems) can't deliver alone. The digital twin bridges that gap by acting as a live traffic control system—always watching, always optimizing.

Predictive Maintenance, Smarter Routing

Warehouse robotics isn't just about movement—it's about reliability. Through continuous tracking of robot behavior—like speed, vibration, or battery cycles—the twin can predict when a robot will need maintenance before it breaks down. This minimizes unplanned downtime and ensures that every part of the system is running at its peak.

At the same time, data from sensors is used to retrain navigation and routing models. If a corridor consistently slows traffic, or if human-machine interactions in a zone lead to delays, the twin adapts, rerouting robots or reassigning tasks to keep operations flowing.

Humans and Machines, Guided by the Same System

Importantly, digital twins aren't about replacing humans. They're about removing friction. In hybrid warehouses, the digital twin doesn't just track machines—it also tracks human workers with the same level of detail (while respecting privacy and safety standards).

- Workers get real-time instructions based on their location
- Robots yield to humans or assist with heavy loads
- Safety zones are monitored and enforced automatically
- Training simulations can be conducted in a virtual replica of the floor

This creates a space where collaboration is fluid—not forced. Where everyone and everything moves with intention, not interference.

From Inventory Hubs to Intelligent Systems

The warehouse has always been a hub of logistics. With digital twins and robotics, it becomes an intelligent ecosystem—self-aware, self-optimizing, and increasingly autonomous. Every sensor, every robot, every shelf becomes part of a larger system that doesn't just react—it thinks.

And as demand for faster delivery and leaner supply chains continues to rise, this level of orchestration will define the winners. Not those who automate the most—but those who coordinate the best. Because in the warehouse of the future, speed alone won't be enough.

Precision wins. Awareness wins. And digital twins make both possible.

Route Optimization and Delivery Forecasting: Precision at the Last Mile

In logistics, the last mile is often the hardest. It's the most unpredictable, the most expensive, and the most visible to the end customer. One wrong turn, one traffic jam, or one missed delivery window can disrupt the entire chain and damage customer satisfaction. This is where digital twins offer a powerful edge—by providing real-time route optimization and delivery forecasting that reacts to what's happening on the ground, not just what's printed on a dispatch schedule.

What used to be a series of static delivery routes and reactive adjustments is now an intelligent, adaptive system—a live simulation of vehicles, packages, weather, traffic, and time.

Dynamic Route Optimization: Smarter Paths, Not Just Faster Ones

Digital twins turn every delivery vehicle into a moving node on a live logistics map. Each van, bike, or drone is tracked in real time, and its route is constantly recalculated based on a wide range of inputs:

- Traffic congestion
- Accidents or road closures
- Weather conditions
- Vehicle performance and fuel/battery levels
- Drop-off complexity (e.g., security access, stairs, time restrictions)
- Delivery priority based on service-level agreements (SLAs)

Rather than following rigid pre-planned routes, drivers are guided dynamically. The system knows not just where they're going, but how best to get there right now—and what stops should be reordered or deferred to stay efficient and on time.

This is especially critical in urban delivery zones, where one blocked intersection or detour can throw off the entire chain. With digital twins feeding off live spatial data, routes are re-optimized minute by minute, ensuring that the fleet operates like a synchronized system—not just a group of vehicles on autopilot.

Forecasting Deliveries with Live Intelligence

Customers expect more than a tracking number—they want accurate, real-time ETAs. Digital twins make that possible by integrating real-time vehicle location, route conditions, and predictive models to forecast delivery windows with far greater precision.

And these forecasts aren't static. If a driver slows down due to construction, the digital twin updates the customer ETA in real time. If a weather system is about to hit a delivery zone, the twin predicts potential delays and automatically notifies logistics teams and customers alike.

This level of visibility and transparency reduces "where's my package?" calls, improves customer trust, and lets service teams focus on exceptions—not chasing answers.

For businesses with tight delivery promises—same-day, next-hour, cold-chain, or high-value products—this kind of predictive clarity isn't just a feature. It's a necessity.

Fleet Coordination and Load Optimization

Digital twins don't just optimize routes—they help coordinate the entire fleet.

- Which vehicle has available capacity for a last-minute pickup nearby?
- Can a return be scheduled into an outbound route without detour?
- Is there an idle vehicle that could be rerouted to handle overflow?
- Will a delivery run exceed the driver's allowed service hours?

The twin sees the full system, not just individual trucks. It balances workloads, minimizes redundancy, and helps logistics managers make better real-time decisions about who goes where, when, and with what.

This results in:

- Fewer wasted miles
- Higher delivery density per route
- Reduced fuel or energy costs

- Improved driver satisfaction due to smoother routing and fewer surprises

Simulation and Stress Testing Before Peak Seasons

Before the holiday rush or a product launch, logistics teams can use digital twins to stress-test the entire delivery network. They simulate spikes in volume, warehouse-to-hub throughput, and delivery region saturation.

- How will the network respond if volume doubles overnight?
- Where are the geographic bottlenecks?
- Which routes require more vehicles, and which can be consolidated?

This turns planning from a guessing game into a modeled scenario with actionable insights. And when real-world volume hits, the system isn't caught off guard—it's already tuned for the load.

From Dispatch to Doorstep: A Smoother Ride

Route optimization and delivery forecasting used to be about reacting to problems after they happened. With digital twins, logistics companies now predict, prevent, and pivot in real time.

They don't just know where packages are. They know where they should be next.

They don't just guess when a delivery will arrive. They calculate it—and recalculate it as conditions change.

They don't just plan routes. They optimize journeys—for time, cost, fuel, and customer experience.

In a world where delivery is a brand promise and time is money, digital twins turn logistics into a precision machine—one that doesn't just move goods, but moves smart.

Combining Human Behavior with Machine Movement: Building Harmony in Hybrid Workspaces

In the race toward automation, it's easy to focus solely on robots, AI, and machines. But the reality on the ground—especially in warehouses, factories, and fulfillment centers—is far more nuanced. Humans and machines are working side by side, sharing space, tasks, and timelines. And without a system to coordinate their interaction, the result can be friction, confusion, or even danger.

That's where digital twins step in—not to replace either party, but to orchestrate the relationship between them. By combining real-time tracking of human behavior with machine movement, digital twins create hybrid environments where people and automation work together safely, efficiently, and intelligently.

Shared Space, Shared Awareness

The challenge in mixed human-machine environments isn't just logistics—it's mutual awareness. A robot doesn't instinctively recognize a distracted worker stepping into its path. And a human can't predict whether an autonomous cart will speed up, slow down, or reverse.

Digital twins solve this by acting as a central nervous system, constantly mapping and interpreting movement—both mechanical and human—within a shared space. This includes:

- Pose detection: Understanding the exact location and orientation of people in 3D space
- Predictive tracking: Projecting movement paths based on current speed and direction
- Contextual reasoning: Differentiating between someone working, resting, or unintentionally entering a restricted zone

- Machine telemetry: Monitoring robot acceleration, planned paths, and task loads

When these data streams converge in the digital twin, the system can predict and prevent collisions, reduce hesitation, and allow for smooth, synchronized activity—even in tight, fast-moving environments.

Use Case: Coordinating Autonomous Robots and Workers

Picture a high-volume fulfillment center. Autonomous mobile robots (AMRs) are moving goods between packing stations while human workers restock shelves, retrieve oversized items, or handle exceptions.

Without coordination, the risks are clear:

- A robot might reroute to avoid a worker, but block another's path
- A worker might unknowingly enter an AMR's blind spot
- Bottlenecks could form in high-traffic zones, with both robots and people waiting for each other to move

With a digital twin, the system sees all of this in real time—and acts accordingly:

- AMRs adjust routes proactively when a worker is nearby
- Workers are alerted to nearby robot activity through smart wearables or visual signals
- Traffic is balanced across the floor, reducing congestion and wait times
- Risk zones are dynamically created and lifted based on live context—not static floor maps

The result is an environment that feels less like a collection of competing workflows and more like a choreographed operation.

Training Machines on Human Patterns

One of the most powerful applications of this integration is when machine behavior is shaped by human patterns. Digital twins don't just track what humans do—they learn from it.

Over time, the system can analyze:

- Which areas are busiest at what times
- How humans naturally approach certain tasks
- Where most near-misses occur between people and machines
- Which routes workers prefer—and why

This insight helps tune robotic behavior to better complement human workflows. For example:

- Robots slow down in human-dense areas—even before someone enters
- Machines avoid known bottlenecks during peak hours
- Task assignments are optimized to prevent crowding or overload
- Machines "learn" the social cues of the floor and adjust accordingly

This human-centric approach to robotics—guided by the digital twin—results in automation that respects context, not just code.

Safety by Design

Perhaps the most immediate benefit of combining human and machine tracking is enhanced safety. Digital twins can enforce safety boundaries intelligently:

- Auto-slowing or pausing robots in real-time as humans enter active zones
- Preventing machines from reactivating unless the twin confirms the area is clear
- Monitoring for unsafe behavior or fatigue indicators in human workers
- Logging near-misses for post-event analysis and future improvement

Rather than relying on fixed barriers or manual overrides, the system provides dynamic safety enforcement—reacting to what's really happening on the floor, not just what's supposed to happen.

Augmenting Human Skill, Not Replacing It

When machines operate in isolation, they're efficient—but rigid. When humans work alone, they're flexible—but prone to error. But when both are coordinated through a digital twin, you get a system that's fast, adaptive, and resilient.

The goal isn't just to make robots smarter. It's to make the entire workplace smarter—where every task is assigned with full awareness of space, skill, and timing. Where machines move with purpose, and humans are empowered—not sidelined—by automation.

This is the future of industrial work: cooperation, not competition. A hybrid world where people and machines are tuned to each other's rhythms, and the digital twin ensures no one steps out of sync.

Retail, logistics, and autonomous systems don't just need data—they need direction. Digital twins provide that, offering a live, evolving map of operations where insight turns into action and action loops back into insight. As these industries push further into automation and real-time responsiveness, the digital twin becomes more than a tool—it becomes the operational core. For companies aiming to stay competitive in a world that doesn't wait, this isn't just innovation. It's survival.

Chapter 12

Healthcare and Human Digital Twins

In healthcare, the stakes are personal. Lives depend on accuracy, timing, and informed decisions. What if doctors could simulate treatments before applying them? What if hospitals could optimize workflows without disrupting care? What if a patient's digital replica—down to the cellular level—could warn of disease before symptoms appear? These aren't futuristic fantasies. They're the emerging reality of human digital twins. This chapter explores how digital twin technology is reshaping healthcare—from hospital systems to personalized medicine—bringing us closer to care that is predictive, precise, and profoundly human.

Personalized Medicine with Heart Modeling: The Barcelona Supercomputing Center Example

In traditional medicine, treatment often begins with averages—what works for most people, most of the time. But no two human bodies are exactly alike. A drug that helps one person might harm another. A surgical procedure that's standard practice could carry hidden risk for someone else. This is the central challenge of modern healthcare: how to treat the individual, not the population.

Enter the concept of the human digital twin—and with it, one of the most compelling real-world breakthroughs: the work being done at the Barcelona Supercomputing Center, where researchers are building digital twins of the human heart.

A Heart That Lives in the Cloud

Using advanced imaging, physics-based modeling, and high-performance computing, the Barcelona team is creating patient-specific digital replicas of human hearts. These are not just anatomical 3D models—they are living simulations, capable of mimicking the electrical, structural, and biochemical behaviors of a real, beating heart.

For a doctor, this changes everything.

- Before prescribing medication for arrhythmia, they can simulate its effect on the patient's exact heart.

- Before a surgeon makes the first incision, they can test different surgical approaches in a digital environment, predicting how the heart will respond.
- Before a condition worsens, doctors can spot changes in the twin—subtle deviations in rhythm, pressure, or blood flow—and intervene early.

It's personalized medicine brought to life, where decisions are based not on general guidelines, but on a patient's unique digital physiology.

How It Works

The process begins with patient data:

- MRI and CT scans provide the structural blueprint
- Electrocardiograms (ECGs) inform electrical activity
- Biomarkers and genetic data add biochemical context
- Machine learning algorithms refine the model, tuning it to the patient's actual responses over time

All this data feeds into a multi-scale simulation, from the cellular level up to organ behavior. This enables clinicians to explore "what-if" scenarios safely, efficiently, and without ever putting the patient at risk.

It's a paradigm shift from reactive care to simulated foresight.

From Diagnosis to Drug Development

Heart twins are just the beginning. As these digital models become more refined and scalable, they have the potential to transform the entire medical journey:

- Diagnosis: Catch abnormalities earlier by watching how the twin evolves
- Treatment planning: Tailor interventions to the patient's real-world complexity
- Rehabilitation: Track recovery virtually and adjust therapy as needed
- Drug testing: Evaluate how a new drug affects different digital hearts before human trials even begin

This technology also opens the door to ethical experimentation. Doctors can test aggressive or high-risk interventions in the twin first—without putting human lives in danger.

The Emotional Power of Seeing Yourself

Beyond the clinical benefits, there's something deeply human about a person being able to see their own heart, beating in real time, in a virtual space. It brings awareness, agency, and even hope.

Imagine telling a patient, "This is your heart. This is how it behaves. Here's what we can do to make it stronger." That's not just care—it's a partnership. A future where patients are participants, not just recipients, in their own healing.

Scaling the Vision

The Barcelona project is a glimpse into the future, but it's also a foundation. As computing becomes more accessible and patient data becomes more integrated, these human digital twins will expand:

- From hearts to lungs, brains, joints, and entire bodies
- From specialty care to primary care and wellness monitoring
- From elite institutions to mainstream hospitals and clinics

The goal isn't just high-tech healthcare. It's high-trust, high-accuracy, personalized medicine, available to everyone—not someday, but soon.

The Barcelona Supercomputing Center has proven that this is possible. A person's heart can now live in both body and code—connected, responsive, and always being watched over by its twin. In a world where every second counts, that's not just innovation.

That's a second chance, built into the system.

Predictive Diagnostics: Seeing Illness Before It Surfaces

In medicine, timing is everything. The earlier you catch a problem, the better the chances of preventing it from becoming life-threatening—or even life-altering. Traditionally, diagnostics have relied on symptoms showing up first. But by the time someone feels pain, experiences fatigue, or notices irregularities, the condition may already be well underway. What if healthcare could flip that equation? What if we could detect illness not just early, but before it even manifests?

That's the promise of predictive diagnostics, and digital twins are making it a reality.

From Detection to Prediction

Digital twins don't wait for symptoms. They're constantly monitoring a patient's data in real time—biometrics, sensor data, wearable inputs, lab results, and historical patterns—comparing it against a live model of how that individual should be functioning. When something begins to drift out of alignment, the twin picks up the subtle signal long before it escalates into something urgent.

Instead of looking for clear signs of disease, the twin looks for deviations from the baseline—small shifts in heart rhythm, blood pressure trends, hormone levels, mobility patterns, or even behavioral cues.

It doesn't say "You're sick."
It says, "Something's off. Let's look into it—now."

How It Works

Predictive diagnostics powered by digital twins rely on three main ingredients:

1. A personalized baseline – The twin understands what's "normal" for that specific individual, not just what's average for the population.

2. Continuous data streams – From wearables, health apps, medical devices, and regular checkups, feeding the twin with up-to-date, contextual data.

3. AI-powered analysis – Machine learning algorithms compare incoming data to millions of past cases, spotting subtle warning signs invisible to the human eye.

The result is a system that's not reactive—it's anticipatory.

A few real-world examples:

- A digital twin notices micro-changes in breathing patterns, paired with elevated resting heart rate and lower sleep quality. It flags potential early-stage respiratory infection—days before the person feels unwell.

- A heart twin spots irregularities in electrical conduction during minor exertion, predicting a future arrhythmia event that would've gone unnoticed on a routine ECG.

- A musculoskeletal twin detects strain imbalance in a runner's gait, flagging risk of injury weeks before a stress fracture develops.

In every case, the alert comes before pain, dysfunction, or permanent damage. That's the true power of a predictive twin—it watches while you live your life, quietly keeping you one step ahead.

Proactive Care, Not Panic

Importantly, predictive diagnostics doesn't mean false alarms and anxiety. The goal isn't to flood people with warnings—it's to contextualize risk and help clinicians act with confidence.

Because the digital twin understands trends over time—not just isolated data points—it can distinguish between natural fluctuations and real threats. It can also suggest targeted next steps:

- "Schedule a stress test."
- "Adjust your sleep or hydration routine."
- "Consider a deeper hormone panel."
- "Increase monitoring for the next 72 hours."

This becomes the foundation for personalized preventive care, where interventions are subtle, early, and effective—before anything becomes critical.

Impact Beyond the Individual

At the population level, predictive diagnostics can transform public health. When anonymized digital twins are aggregated, health systems can:

- Identify rising trends (e.g., flu outbreaks or environmental triggers)
- Forecast hospital admission rates
- Allocate resources more intelligently
- Model long-term outcomes based on lifestyle changes or community interventions

Instead of reacting to waves of illness, health systems can get ahead of them, easing strain on infrastructure and improving outcomes across the board.

Medicine That Looks Forward

The future of healthcare isn't just about more tests or faster scans. It's about knowing before showing—about catching the signal before the symptom. With predictive diagnostics, powered by human digital twins, care becomes proactive, efficient, and deeply personal.

You don't wait to get sick.
You get a heads-up while you're still healthy.
And that heads-up might be the difference between managing a risk and facing a crisis.

This is where digital twins shine—not just in critical care or complex surgery, but in the quiet, invisible moments where disease begins. And in those moments, prevention becomes the most powerful treatment of all.

Simulation-Based Surgery and Training: Practice, Precision, and Preparedness

Surgeons don't get do-overs. Every cut matters. Every decision is final. In high-risk procedures, even the most experienced hands carry the burden of unpredictability—because every patient is different, and no two surgeries are exactly the same. But what if a surgeon could rehearse the procedure—not just on a generic model, but on the patient's own anatomy, with all its unique nuances, challenges, and risks? What if training no longer relied solely on cadavers, textbooks, or observation, but on immersive, real-time digital twins?

Simulation-based surgery, powered by human digital twins, is bringing this possibility to life. It's turning surgery from a high-stakes performance into a well-practiced plan.

From Textbook to Twin: Rehearsing the Real

Traditional surgical training relies heavily on repetition, observation, and generalized anatomy. But no one learns to fly by watching someone else do it—they learn in a flight simulator. Digital twins are now providing the medical equivalent: a real-time, responsive surgical simulation environment based on the actual patient's data.

Here's how it works:

- Medical imaging (MRI, CT, ultrasound) is used to create a 3D model of the patient's anatomy—organs, tissues, vessels, and all.

- The model is enhanced with physics-based behavior, so it reacts like living tissue—stretching, bleeding, pulsing.
- Surgeons interact with the twin in a virtual or augmented reality environment, using real instruments or haptic feedback systems.
- They can simulate every step of the procedure: the incision, the tool trajectory, the tissue response—even unexpected complications.
- The twin records performance, timing, pressure, angles, and outcomes—providing immediate feedback and improvement loops.

The result? Surgeons walk into the OR with muscle memory, foresight, and clarity. Not just because they've practiced—but because they've practiced on that patient's unique body.

Precision That Saves Lives

Simulation-based surgery doesn't just improve confidence. It reduces risk:

- Fewer surprises during surgery
- Shorter operation times
- Lower complication rates
- Better outcomes for patients with complex or rare conditions

In trauma surgery, where time is everything, knowing the exact vessel path or organ structure in advance can make the difference between life and death. For tumor removal, being able to simulate proximity to critical nerves or blood flow allows for maximally effective, minimally invasive procedures.

This is no longer science fiction—it's happening in leading hospitals and training institutions today. The technology is rapidly advancing, and it's being integrated not just into elite cases, but into the standard surgical workflow.

Elevating Medical Training

Beyond the operating room, simulation-based digital twins are revolutionizing how surgeons, nurses, and medical students learn.

- Trainees can repeat procedures endlessly in a virtual environment
- Errors can be safely explored and learned from
- Rare and complex surgeries can be experienced before they're ever encountered in real life
- Performance data can be tracked over time to measure growth and pinpoint areas of improvement

Imagine a surgical resident practicing a liver resection 100 times before ever touching a patient—adjusting for different anatomies, bleeding risks, or tumor types. They enter the OR not as a beginner, but as someone who's already walked through the steps over and over—with guidance, correction, and clarity.

This levels the playing field for training across regions, institutions, and access levels. It also ensures that experience isn't limited by opportunity—it's accelerated by technology.

Training for the Unpredictable

Perhaps the most powerful element of simulation is its ability to prepare for the unexpected.

- What happens if the artery ruptures mid-procedure?
- What if the patient's blood pressure drops suddenly?
- How do you react to an allergic reaction during anesthesia?

These can all be modeled in advance. Teams can run emergency drills, rehearse response protocols, and ensure collaboration under pressure. In real life, there's no pause button. But in the digital twin, there is—and with it, the ability to learn faster, safer, and smarter.

Human Skill, Digitally Enhanced

Digital twins aren't replacing surgeons. They're making them better. More prepared. More precise. More capable of delivering exceptional care, even in the most complex scenarios.

They extend far beyond the screen. They translate into steadier hands, sharper instincts, and more lives saved.

Because when it comes to surgery, you don't get to rewind.
But now, with simulation-based training, you get to rehearse—again and again—until doing it right feels like second nature.
And in medicine, that second nature could save a life.

Ethical Concerns: Data, Consent, and the Edges of AI in Healthcare

As powerful as digital twins are in healthcare, they walk a tightrope between innovation and intrusion. When you model the human body in exacting detail, when AI starts to predict illness before symptoms appear, when virtual replicas simulate surgeries and suggest interventions—you're not just managing data. You're managing trust.

Digital twins thrive on data. But in medicine, data isn't just a resource—it's personal. Every heartbeat, hormone level, genetic marker, and behavioral pattern represents someone's identity, history, and future. With this level of detail, ethical questions don't just arise—they demand answers.

The Data Dilemma: How Much Is Too Much?

For a digital twin to function well, it needs comprehensive, often continuous data—from medical records to wearables, imaging scans to voice notes, even real-time sensor streams from inside hospital rooms or homes. And the more connected the twin becomes, the more vulnerable that data is.

Key concerns include:

- Security: Can this data be hacked, leaked, or misused?
- Ownership: Does the patient truly control their digital twin? Or does the hospital, tech vendor, or insurer?
- Scope: What happens when data collected for health purposes is used to assess credit, insurance rates, or employment risk?

Without robust privacy frameworks and patient-first policies, digital twins risk becoming a form of digital overreach—collecting more than necessary, storing longer than needed, and being used in ways the patient never agreed to.

Informed Consent in the Age of AI

Consent isn't a checkbox. It's a process of understanding. But in a world where twins continuously learn, evolve, and act semi-autonomously, traditional consent models start to break down.

- Does a patient understand how their data will be used, now and in the future?
- Are they notified when AI makes a recommendation on their behalf?
- Can they opt out of data collection without losing access to care?
- Do they have visibility into how their twin is being updated or accessed?

Informed consent must evolve to match the complexity and speed of digital twins. That means giving patients real-time control over their data, transparency into system logic, and the right to revoke access—not as a legal form, but as a living part of their health experience.

When AI Crosses the Line

Perhaps the most debated concern is AI overreach—when the system stops supporting decisions and starts making them.

Digital twins powered by AI can recommend treatments, flag anomalies, or suggest early interventions. But what happens when:

- An algorithm suggests a course of action a doctor disagrees with?
- A system prioritizes patients based on cost-efficiency over need?
- A hospital automates care decisions based on digital models without human review?

These aren't hypotheticals. As AI-driven twins become more advanced, they could nudge or override human judgment—not through malice, but through confidence in their own predictions.

This raises ethical red flags:

- Who's accountable if the twin is wrong?
- Should machines make life-altering choices without human context?
- Can a system be biased—even if it's built on real-world data?

Bias, after all, isn't neutralized by data volume. In fact, the more historical data a twin uses, the more likely it reflects existing inequities in care—from racial disparities to gender bias to regional gaps in access.

Without strict oversight, AI-driven twins risk becoming amplifiers of injustice, rather than tools for equity.

Building Ethics into the Code

To harness the full potential of digital twins while protecting human dignity, the healthcare industry must adopt ethics by design. That means:

- Transparent algorithms: Patients and providers should know how decisions are made.
- Explainable AI: Systems must justify their recommendations in clear, human terms.
- Patient sovereignty: The twin belongs to the person it represents—full stop.
- Oversight frameworks: Cross-disciplinary boards (clinicians, ethicists, technologists, patients) should monitor how twins are built and used.
- Data minimization: Use only what's necessary, keep it only as long as needed, and anonymize where possible.

Ethics shouldn't be a footnote. It should be embedded in every layer of digital twin development—from system design to clinical implementation.

The Twin Must Serve, Not Replace

At its best, the human digital twin enhances trust. It brings clarity, foresight, and personalized care. But without clear boundaries, it can do the opposite—creating uncertainty, intrusion, or fear.

The goal isn't to slow innovation. It's to shape it with intention.

A digital twin should be a mirror, not a master. A partner in care, not a silent authority. A bridge between patient and provider—not a gatekeeper.

Because when technology reflects who we are, we must ensure it also reflects what we value. Privacy. Consent. Equity. And above all—human agency.

How Digital Twins Could Extend Life or Quality of Care: From Reactive Treatment to Lifelong Partnership

At the heart of digital twin technology in healthcare is a quietly radical promise: not just to treat illness, but to extend life and enhance the quality of living. It's a shift from managing disease to maintaining health. From episodic care to continuous insight. From looking at what's wrong to understanding why, when, and how it started—before it becomes irreversible.

This isn't a distant vision. It's beginning now, in fragments—heart models in Barcelona, predictive diagnostics in smart clinics, surgery simulations in leading hospitals. The momentum is building. The question isn't whether digital twins will transform healthcare—it's how far we'll let them go.

From Early Detection to Lifelong Prevention

One of the clearest ways digital twins can extend life is by catching problems before they escalate. We've already seen how predictive diagnostics can flag anomalies before symptoms show. But when that predictive capacity is woven into a lifelong model—constantly updated, personalized, and refined—prevention becomes a living system.

- A digital twin sees patterns others miss: the slow drift in kidney function, the subtle signs of pre-diabetes, the early shifts in gait that hint at neurological decline.

- It alerts care teams early, helping patients make lifestyle adjustments while it still matters.
- Over time, the twin becomes not just a tool—but a health ally, watching quietly in the background, always learning.

That's how life is extended—not just by intervening in emergencies, but by avoiding them altogether.

Empowering Chronic Care Management

For patients living with chronic conditions—diabetes, heart disease, autoimmune disorders, cancer recovery—everyday management is exhausting. Medications. Appointments. Monitoring. The fear of the unknown. A digital twin changes that.

By mirroring the individual's body and condition in real time, the twin:

- Flags flare-ups before they peak
- Recommends treatment adjustments based on how the body responds—not generic protocols
- Tracks fatigue, movement, food intake, and environmental factors to build personalized care loops
- Reduces unnecessary visits by handling more care virtually, but with confidence

This results in fewer hospitalizations, fewer medication missteps, and better control—not through more intervention, but through smarter, more precise care.

And more than that, it offers peace of mind. For patients managing long-term illness, just knowing the twin is watching means they can live without constantly worrying about what's next.

Enhanced Quality of Life, Not Just More Years

Extending life isn't just about adding years to a timeline—it's about adding freedom, clarity, and comfort to those years. Digital twins do this in subtle but powerful ways:

- Helping elderly patients stay independent longer, with smart fall detection and environment-aware assistance
- Supporting mental health by monitoring sleep, activity, mood indicators, and providing proactive check-ins
- Enabling more dignified end-of-life care by helping teams simulate care plans and prepare for what's ahead
- Giving caregivers tools to support without micromanaging—alerting them only when needed

When technology adapts to people—instead of the other way around—quality of life improves naturally. And that's where the twin becomes less of a tool, and more of a companion.

A Living Medical Record, Always in Context

Over a lifetime, a person's health story becomes scattered—different doctors, different systems, different charts. Important details get lost, context is missed, and treatment becomes reactive instead of responsive.

A digital twin unifies that story.

It becomes a central, dynamic representation of the person—not just their records, but their trends, risks, preferences, and outcomes. New doctors don't start from scratch. Emergency teams don't guess. Long-term plans are informed by everything that came before—in context.

This continuity isn't just convenient—it's lifesaving. It turns one-off encounters into a continuous care experience, no matter where the patient is or who's treating them.

The Next Horizon: Human Longevity

Researchers are already exploring how digital twins might push the boundaries of human longevity:

- Simulating aging at the cellular level to understand how to slow or reverse it

- Modeling organ function to test therapies before damage accumulates
- Pairing genetics with real-world behavior to predict and modify lifespan influencers
- Running complex simulations of drug combinations for age-related conditions without the need for trial-and-error in humans

With this level of foresight and personalization, the focus shifts from fighting disease to preserving vitality.

We won't just live longer—we'll live longer well.

From Health Records to Health Guardians

The digital twin doesn't forget. It doesn't overlook trends. It doesn't need to wait for symptoms. And it never stops working. Over time, it becomes something new in the world of medicine: a digital health guardian—one that knows you, learns with you, and helps you make choices that matter.

This is how we extend life.
By extending understanding.
By extending control.
And by extending care into the quiet moments, long before anyone knows they're at risk.

Digital twins don't replace doctors. They amplify care—quietly, consistently, and, in time, perhaps lifesavingly.

Digital twins are giving healthcare what it's long needed: foresight. By mirroring the body, simulating treatments, and modeling hospital operations in real time, they're turning guesswork into guided care. From preventing surgical errors to forecasting chronic conditions, digital twins are becoming quiet partners in healing—working in the background, constantly learning, and empowering clinicians to do what they do best: care. The future of medicine isn't just more advanced—it's more personal. And the twin makes it possible.

PART IV

STRATEGY, ETHICS, AND THE FUTURE

Chapter 13

How to Start—And Scale

For all the potential digital twins offer, the biggest question most businesses face is simple: Where do we begin? The technology is powerful, but it doesn't have to be overwhelming. Whether you're in manufacturing, logistics, healthcare, or urban infrastructure, getting started with digital twins isn't about building a perfect model on day one—it's about building momentum. This chapter lays out the practical path forward: how to pilot, prove value, and scale responsibly. Because innovation doesn't start with complexity. It starts with clarity and the right first move.

Audit What Data You Already Have: Your Digital Twin May Already Be Half Built

Before you invest in new tools, sensors, or platforms, take a hard look at what's already in front of you. Most organizations—whether they realize it or not—are already sitting on a goldmine of data. Machines that log outputs, systems that track inventory, sensors embedded in infrastructure, digital maintenance records, even spreadsheets updated manually every day. It may not be polished, but it's a start.

The first step toward building a digital twin isn't installing new tech—it's auditing the data you already have.

Look Across, Not Just Down

Start by surveying all departments. Manufacturing, logistics, operations, IT, safety, compliance—each may be running their own systems, quietly collecting streams of data that have never been connected. Ask:

- What systems do we use for monitoring and reporting?
- What sensors or IoT devices are already active?
- What historical data exists in ERP, CRM, WMS, or SCADA systems?
- Are there cameras, temperature gauges, GPS trackers, or badge readers in use?
- Do we have spreadsheets or dashboards tracking performance or usage manually?

You may find more than expected: camera footage, time-stamped event logs, GPS routes, maintenance histories, or environmental sensor outputs. All of these are inputs your digital twin can ingest and learn from.

Identify Gaps—and Opportunities

Once you map what you have, the next step is to identify what's missing. This isn't about finding flaws—it's about understanding the limits of your current visibility.

- Do you know where things are, but not how they behave over time?
- Do you get alerts, but no predictive trends?
- Can you see individual system performance, but not how they interact?

Gaps don't mean you're behind—they highlight where small investments can unlock big returns. For instance, adding low-cost sensors to critical machinery may open up real-time monitoring. Integrating location data may enable spatial modeling. Layering timestamps onto event logs can turn basic records into process simulations.

Clean and Standardize

Raw data is only as useful as it is usable. Many organizations struggle not because they lack data, but because it's inconsistent, siloed, or unstructured. Before building a digital twin, invest time in cleaning, organizing, and standardizing your datasets.

- Use consistent units of measurement (e.g., meters, seconds, Celsius)

- Align timestamps across systems (ideally using NTP or GPS sync)
- Eliminate duplicate or redundant data sources
- Structure historical records in formats that analytics platforms can ingest

This stage may not be flashy, but it's foundational. A digital twin thrives on clarity and consistency—and your existing data, once cleaned, may get you 60–70% of the way to a functional model.

Connect, Don't Rebuild

You don't need to scrap your legacy systems to build a digital twin. In fact, one of the most powerful strategies is to connect existing tools into a shared framework.

Digital twins aren't meant to replace your systems—they're meant to unify them. By tapping into APIs, existing databases, or streaming feeds, you can bring scattered data into a central, real-time model without massive disruption.

This approach lowers cost, speeds implementation, and ensures the twin reflects your actual workflows—not some idealized version that never matches reality.

The Value Is Already There—Now Unlock It

Auditing your data isn't just a checklist—it's an eye-opening process. It helps your teams see the value they've already created, often without realizing it. It also builds momentum and confidence. Instead of starting from zero, you're starting from a strong foundation.

And that changes the conversation from "How do we start?" to "What can we do next?"

In most cases, the answer is right there in your files, your feeds, and your logs—waiting to be connected, cleaned, and brought to life in the form of a digital twin.

Because often, your next big innovation isn't out there.
It's already in-house.
You just need to see it differently.

Use Existing Frameworks (USD, Scene Graphs): Don't Reinvent the Wheel—Stand on It

One of the biggest mistakes organizations make when starting with digital twins is trying to build everything from scratch. It's understandable—there's pressure to be custom, scalable, proprietary. But the reality is, much of the groundwork has already been laid. Years of progress in 3D rendering, gaming engines, and visual effects have given us a set of mature, powerful frameworks designed to model complex, interactive environments. And now, those same tools are being used to power digital twins—not just in entertainment, but in factories, hospitals, cities, and enterprise systems.

If you want to move fast, integrate easily, and scale smart, don't build the foundation. Use one.

USD: The Universal Scene Description Format

Developed by Pixar, USD (Universal Scene Description) was originally designed to handle massive, complex 3D animation environments. But it's become one of the most important open standards for organizing and sharing scene data across systems—especially where collaboration, layering, and flexibility matter.

In the context of digital twins, USD offers:

- Modularity: Easily break environments into components (e.g., machines, rooms, buildings)
- Versioning and overrides: Update individual elements without disrupting the whole system
- Multi-user workflows: Engineers, designers, analysts can all work on the same model from different perspectives
- Interoperability: USD plays well with major 3D tools, game engines, and simulation platforms

If your digital twin involves 3D space, live updates, and multiple data sources, USD gives you a battle-tested foundation for managing it all.

Scene Graphs: The Structural Backbone of Spatial Intelligence

A scene graph is a hierarchical structure used to organize and manage all the elements within a 3D or spatial scene—objects, their properties, and their relationships. It tells your system what's in the space, where it is, and how it's connected to everything else.

Think of it as the skeleton of your digital twin's brain.

With scene graphs, you can:

- Track spatial relationships: Which object is near which? What moves with what?
- Manage dependencies: When a conveyor belt moves, what happens to the boxes on it?
- Simulate visibility and interaction: Can this robot "see" that obstacle? Can a human reach this lever?
- Build dynamic behavior: If a sensor detects motion, trigger a visual alert, reroute a robot, or flag a potential safety issue

In industries like manufacturing, logistics, and smart cities, scene graphs are what make real-time digital twins responsive, logical, and scalable.

Why These Frameworks Matter

Without a common format like USD or a structure like a scene graph, your digital twin becomes a tangled mess of systems—each talking in its own language, interpreting space differently, and failing to share context.

- One camera tracks objects in pixels
- One sensor logs motion in meters
- A dashboard interprets data in time slices
- A robot navigates using a separate map

This disconnect kills real-time coordination.

But with shared frameworks, everything—vision systems, simulation engines, AI models, and human interfaces—plugs into the same core structure. It's not just about efficiency. It's about making the system think as one.

Real-World Success: Gaming Tech Meets Industrial Scale

Intel's Scenescape platform and other leading digital twin solutions are already leveraging these frameworks.

Rather than building a custom visualization or spatial logic engine from scratch, they adapt proven tools from the gaming industry:

- Game engines like Unreal and Unity for high-fidelity visualization
- USD and GLTF for object modeling and scene description
- Scene graphs to manage relationships and behaviors
- Real-time rendering pipelines to display and simulate complex environments at scale

This isn't a shortcut. It's best practice. These tools have already been stress-tested in environments that demand high performance, real-time interactivity, and complex asset management.

Build on What Works, Focus on What Matters

By adopting existing frameworks, you don't just save time—you free up resources to focus on what actually differentiates your twin:

- The behaviors that matter to your operations
- The KPIs your teams track
- The AI models that match your environment
- The decisions that shape your business

You build smarter, faster, and with fewer surprises. And when you scale, you're standing on platforms designed to handle growth—built by global communities with decades of experience.

Because in digital twin development, the smartest move isn't always building more.
It's building better—on top of what's already solid.

Choose a Test Case with High Value and Low Complexity: Start Small, Win Big

The key to successfully implementing a digital twin isn't ambition—it's traction. Trying to model your entire operation out of the gate is a fast track to budget overruns, technical debt, and frustrated teams. The smarter path? Start with one problem. One process. One environment. The goal is to prove value early and clearly, with minimal risk.

That's why your first digital twin use case should be high value but low complexity. A tightly scoped scenario that's easy to define, quick to implement, and highly visible in its impact. Because once people see it working, momentum builds fast.

Why This Approach Works

Think of your first use case as a live demo for your organization—a small-scale proof that digital twins aren't just buzzwords, but a tangible, repeatable solution to real problems.

Choosing a lightweight, high-reward target helps you:

- Minimize risk: Fewer systems to connect, fewer people to coordinate.
- Accelerate timelines: Show value in weeks or months—not years.
- Build internal champions: Teams who benefit early become advocates.
- Create a feedback loop: Learn what works and what doesn't before scaling.
- Unlock budget: Nothing secures funding like proven ROI.

This is how adoption takes root—not through sweeping digital transformation plans, but through tactical wins that inspire confidence.

What Makes a Great First Use Case?

You're looking for something with:

■ Clear business impact: Can it cut costs, reduce downtime, boost efficiency, or improve safety?

■ Narrow technical scope: Does it require minimal integration to get started?

■ Readily available data: Do sensors already exist? Can the twin be powered by existing systems?

■ Actionable outcomes: Will the insights lead to real decisions or improvements?

■ Stakeholder visibility: Will its success be noticed by leadership, frontline teams, or customers?

Real-World Examples of Strong Starter Twins

- Manufacturing: Monitor a single high-maintenance machine to reduce unplanned downtime. Use existing IoT data to predict wear and optimize service schedules.

- Logistics: Digitize one warehouse zone to track item movement and robot/human flow. Use pose detection to improve safety and efficiency.

- Retail: Model foot traffic in a key store location to optimize layout, staffing, and energy usage. Use camera data and basic spatial mapping.

- Smart cities: Pilot traffic flow optimization at one congested intersection using digital twin simulation based on real-time feeds.

- Healthcare: Create a digital twin of one operating room to track equipment usage and sterilization cycles, improving turnaround and reducing risk.

Each of these examples is tangible, targeted, and tied to a measurable outcome. They don't require modeling an entire factory, campus, or city—but they showcase the core value of the twin concept.

Don't Wait for Perfect—Start With Practical

Waiting for the perfect use case often means never starting at all. But choosing a focused, strategic scenario that's small enough to build fast and big enough to matter is how successful digital twin programs begin.

Your first implementation doesn't have to be flashy. It just has to work. And when it does, it becomes proof—for your team, your leadership, and your future—that the twin isn't theoretical.

It's practical. It's scalable.
And it's ready to deliver value right now.

Cross-Department Collaboration: Build a Twin, Not a Silo

One of the most powerful things a digital twin can do is break down barriers—between departments, systems, and ways of thinking. But to do that, it has to be built with collaboration in mind. If your digital twin only serves one team's goals, using one set of data, managed by one department, it's not a twin. It's a fancy mirror.

To unlock the real value, you need cross-functional alignment from day one. Because the insight a digital twin generates in one part of the business is often only useful when it's connected to another.

Why Collaboration Matters

- Operations may track performance, but don't always understand system dependencies.
- IT owns the infrastructure, but may not know which insights are most urgent on the ground.
- Engineering designs the systems, but doesn't see how they behave in real-time use.
- Leadership wants visibility, but needs help interpreting it into decisions.

When these groups work together, the twin becomes a shared asset—not a departmental tool.

Use the twin to align around shared goals, like reducing downtime, improving safety, streamlining customer experience, or forecasting demand more accurately. You're not just connecting data streams—you're connecting teams around the same digital representation of reality.

Best Practices for Cross-Department Collaboration

- Involve stakeholders early: Don't wait until the rollout to bring in other teams. Loop in users, decision-makers, and frontline staff from the planning stage.

- Create a governance structure: Define who owns what—data, permissions, outcomes—and who needs access to what.

- Define shared KPIs: Make sure different departments aren't pulling the twin in different directions. Agree on what success looks like.

- Start with a use case that touches multiple teams: For example, reducing delivery time might involve logistics, customer service, and IT.

- Document and communicate learnings: Let everyone see what the twin is teaching you, not just the team that initiated it.

The goal? A twin that reflects not just systems—but the way your organization really works.

Pitfalls to Avoid: Lessons from the Field

Digital twins are a powerful concept—but implementation is where things go wrong if you're not careful. Here are some of the most common mistakes, and how to steer clear of them:

1. Isolated Pilots with No Path to Scale

A small pilot is a great starting point—if it leads somewhere. Too often, teams run isolated experiments that never connect to broader systems or strategies.

Avoid this by:
- Choosing a pilot with clear connections to larger operations
- Documenting every lesson, challenge, and result
- Building a roadmap from day one that links pilot success to broader rollout

2. Vendor Lock-In

Many vendors offer powerful digital twin platforms—but some trap you in closed ecosystems that limit your flexibility. This can lead to escalating costs, limited interoperability, and difficulty adapting as your needs evolve.

Avoid this by:
- Prioritizing open standards (e.g., USD, GLTF, APIs)
- Asking hard questions about data ownership and exportability
- Ensuring you can integrate new tools and scale without being boxed in

3. Overbuilding Too Early

Trying to model everything at once often leads to complexity, delays, and burnout. Not everything needs to be modeled in 3D or tracked in real time.

Avoid this by:
- Scoping tightly and focusing on value, not visual wow
- Adding complexity only as ROI becomes clear
- Starting with just enough fidelity to answer key questions

4. Tech-First Thinking

A digital twin is a means to an end, not the end itself. Chasing features or trying to use every available sensor or data point can lead to bloated systems that don't solve meaningful problems.

Avoid this by:
- Starting with the business case, not the tech stack
- Working backward from the decision or insight you want to enable
- Involving non-technical stakeholders who can anchor the project in real-world needs

5. Neglecting Change Management

Digital twins often surface operational truths that make people uncomfortable—inefficiencies, safety risks, or underused assets. If teams aren't prepared for what the twin reveals, they may resist its insights.

Avoid this by:
- Framing the twin as a tool for improvement, not punishment
- Creating feedback loops with users and operators
- Recognizing and rewarding behaviors that align with data-informed improvements

Build Together, Scale Together

The real power of a digital twin isn't just in what it models—it's in how it helps people see their work differently. But that only happens when multiple departments contribute, share, and benefit.

And the real risk isn't just technical. It's organizational—spending time, money, and momentum on a twin that no one else can use, expand, or trust.

So build smart. Build open. Build together.
Because a digital twin isn't just a tool.
It's a shared source of truth—and its impact grows with every person it connects.

How Intel and Mevea Started with Side Projects: Big Innovation from Small Beginnings

It's easy to look at industry leaders like Intel and Mevea today—delivering cutting-edge digital twin platforms used in cities, factories, and hospitals—and assume they got there with massive budgets and top-down mandates. But the truth is far more relatable—and more encouraging.

Both companies started their digital twin journeys not with fanfare, but with curiosity, experimentation, and side projects. Their success wasn't born in boardrooms. It started with small teams solving real problems, proving value quietly, and scaling only after results were undeniable.

Intel: From a Passion Project to a Platform

Intel's Scenescape wasn't rolled out as a flagship product overnight. It began as an after-hours project—driven by a small team asking a deceptively simple question: What if we could make machines and sensors actually understand the world around them in 3D?

With a physics and engineering background, the developers behind Scenescape weren't satisfied with how traditional AI models simply labeled objects in 2D images. They wanted to add context, pose, and space—to not only know what was detected, but where it was, how it was moving, and what might happen next.

They started small:

- Calibrating cameras to detect real-world position and orientation
- Projecting sensor data into spatial environments
- Building rough, internal demos to show how two systems could communicate if they shared a spatial map

What they were building wasn't called a "digital twin" at first—it was just a better way to understand machine environments. But the pieces were all there.

Over time, the project gained traction. It proved its worth in safety-critical scenarios. Teams saw its value across different industries—from retail to manufacturing to healthcare. And eventually, what began as a side project evolved into Intel Scenescape, a full-fledged platform used by enterprise clients to create real-time, spatially aware digital twins.

The lesson? Don't wait for a directive—build what matters. Show, don't sell. Innovation thrives when people chase real problems with real passion.

Mevea: Engineering the Twin from Simulation Roots

Finland-based Mevea also didn't set out to build the next big thing in digital twins. Their roots were in simulation and virtual prototyping—helping manufacturers test complex machines before building them physically. For years, they focused on high-fidelity, physics-based simulations of excavators, cranes, and other heavy machinery.

But over time, their clients started asking:
What if we could use these virtual models during operation?
What if we could keep learning from the machine after it leaves the factory?

That curiosity sparked something bigger.

Mevea didn't try to reinvent the wheel. They took the simulation models they already had and layered on live data feeds. They connected real control systems to their virtual environments. They turned machines into living systems that could be tested, trained on, and optimized throughout their lifecycle.

Their twin wasn't a product launch—it was an extension of a capability they were already delivering. It was organic, grounded in client needs, and built step-by-step with feedback from real users.

Today, Mevea's digital twins are used not just for prototyping, but for operator training, product improvement, maintenance simulation, and real-world machine behavior tracking. But none of it started with a grand transformation. It started with listening—and iterating.

Why These Origin Stories Matter

Intel and Mevea's paths reveal a powerful truth: Digital twin success doesn't require massive investment or sweeping change at the start. It just requires solving a real problem—cleverly, persistently, and with a willingness to build sideways before scaling upward.

This is a blueprint any business can follow:

- Start with an internal friction point, not an external mandate.
- Let small teams tinker. Give them space to try.
- Don't wait for executive buy-in to prove value—use results to earn it.
- Build on what you already know or already have.
- Connect ideas across disciplines—physics, AI, IT, operations.

These aren't "tech company" strategies. They're human strategies—rooted in curiosity, collaboration, and courage to explore the edge of what's possible.

Because the next breakthrough in your organization may not come from a strategy session.
It might come from someone staying late.
Solving a problem no one else noticed.
And quietly building the foundation for your future digital twin—one line of code, one experiment, one insight at a time.

Digital twins are no longer experimental—they're essential. But success doesn't come from adopting them all at once. It comes from starting with purpose, proving value in specific use cases, and scaling based on results. The most impactful digital twin strategies don't chase hype—they solve real problems, one connected system at a time. Whether you're tracking machines, managing supply chains, optimizing environments, or modeling human health, the approach is the same: start small, think big, scale smart. The future is already moving—and the twin is how you move with it.

Chapter 14

Ethics, Privacy, and Responsible Deployment

The more accurate and intelligent digital twins become, the more they reflect not just systems and machines—but people, behaviors, and choices. With that comes a tension that businesses can't afford to ignore: how to harness this power without crossing ethical lines. As virtual replicas grow more detailed, more connected, and more predictive, they raise real questions about consent, surveillance, ownership, and control. This chapter doesn't chase hypotheticals. It focuses on the very real decisions companies are already facing and the consequences of getting them wrong—or right.

Surveillance vs. Insight

There's a fine line between seeing clearly and watching too closely. Digital twins offer visibility that once felt like science fiction—real-time, data-driven reflections of people, environments, and systems. That kind of power can lead to breakthroughs in efficiency, safety, and convenience. But it can just as easily tip into something more uncomfortable: constant surveillance dressed up as innovation.

It starts with intent. When a company builds a digital twin of a workspace, for example, are they doing it to improve layout, reduce energy waste, and streamline logistics? Or are they quietly monitoring employee movements to track productivity, behavior, and even bathroom breaks? Both use similar technology. Both may rely on spatial awareness, sensor fusion, and behavioral modeling. But the outcomes—and more importantly, how people feel about those outcomes—couldn't be more different.

Insight is about clarity. It helps businesses understand the flow of their operations, identify friction points, and make better decisions. When done right, it's visible, transparent, and beneficial to all parties involved. A retailer using foot traffic data to redesign store layouts, for instance, might boost sales and make the space more enjoyable for customers at the same time. That's insight.

Surveillance, on the other hand, is hidden. It's data collection without clear communication, often without consent, and usually skewed toward control rather than collaboration. It breeds mistrust. It positions people as problems to be managed rather than participants in a shared system. And in an era where privacy is already under constant pressure, that distinction matters more than ever.

The technology itself doesn't have an opinion. A spatial camera doesn't decide whether it's being used for safety or scrutiny. But humans do. Business leaders, developers, product managers—anyone building or deploying digital twins holds that responsibility. And it's not always black and white. There are gray areas where value and intrusion overlap.

Take smart buildings. A digital twin of an office tower might be designed to manage lighting, heating, and elevator usage more efficiently. But what happens when that system starts logging which employees arrive late, who takes the stairs, or who gathers in certain areas? It's a slippery slope. The line between optimization and oversight isn't just technical—it's cultural and ethical.

One of the most important steps a company can take is to define the purpose of its digital twin initiative upfront. What are you trying to understand? What are you hoping to change? Who benefits from the data being collected? And crucially—who gets a say in how it's used?

Insight becomes meaningful when it's shared. When employees know they're part of a system designed to support them, not spy on them, they're more likely to engage with it. Transparency turns technology into a partnership. It invites feedback, fosters trust, and opens the door to improvements that serve everyone.

Surveillance erodes that trust. It sends the message that people aren't trusted to do their jobs without digital oversight. Over time, that kind of environment creates tension, resentment, and resistance—not innovation.

There's also the question of scale. A small team using digital twins to monitor a machine shop is one thing. A multinational corporation using them to track every motion inside its facilities across multiple continents is another. The bigger the system, the greater the risk of disconnect—between leadership and workers, between intent and perception, between what's legal and what's ethical.

Laws often lag behind technology. In many regions, there's little regulation around how workplace data is collected and used. That doesn't mean businesses have a blank check. On the contrary, those moving first in the digital twin space have a chance to set the tone—proving that visibility can coexist with respect, and that data doesn't have to come at the cost of dignity.

This matters because digital twins are only becoming more intelligent. As AI models improve, these systems aren't just mirroring behavior—they're starting to predict it. What happens when a system flags a worker as "inefficient" based on a flawed model or biased data? What recourse does that person have? What kind of workplace are we building when human judgment is increasingly handed over to algorithms?

The point isn't to avoid technology. It's to use it responsibly. Insight can empower people. It can make their jobs easier, safer, and more rewarding. Surveillance, on the other hand, turns those same tools into levers of pressure and control. The technology is the same. The impact is not.

It comes down to values. Companies that center their digital twin strategies on trust, inclusion, and transparency won't just avoid ethical landmines—they'll unlock deeper, more sustainable forms of value. Because people support what they understand. They respect systems that respect them back.

Surveillance might get short-term compliance. Insight builds long-term alignment.

Data Ownership and User Consent

If data is the lifeblood of a digital twin, then ownership is its pulse. Who controls that data? Who has the right to access it, use it, profit from it—or even erase it? These questions are no longer abstract. As digital twins become more intertwined with people's daily lives, from factory floors to hospital rooms, the answers carry real weight. And when the system involves human behavior or biometric inputs, consent isn't optional—it's foundational.

The truth is, most people have no idea how much data they generate. Every step tracked by a sensor, every facial recognition hit from a camera, every log file from a wearable device—it all feeds into a bigger picture that's often invisible to the person it represents. In digital twin environments, that picture can be startlingly complete. It's not just about what you did, but where, when, how often, and sometimes even why.

That kind of precision demands a level of respect most systems today aren't designed for. It's one thing to ask users to click "I agree" on a terms-of-service page. It's another to offer real agency over how their data is collected, modeled, and applied. In too many deployments, the flow of information is one-way. People provide the data—voluntarily or not—and the system acts on it without ever circling back.

That's where trust starts to break down.

In a factory using digital twins to improve workflow, workers may not object to sensors tracking machine usage. But if those same sensors start analyzing posture, eye movement, or break times, without clear communication or choice, things get murky. It's not about being anti-technology—it's about wanting clarity on where the boundaries are.

The principle of informed consent is supposed to set those boundaries. It's the idea that people should know what data is being collected, why it's being collected, who has access to it, and how it will be used. But in practice, consent is often buried in legalese, treated as a checkbox rather than a conversation. That doesn't hold up in a world where digital twins can mirror not just environments, but individuals—down to their heartbeat, behavior patterns, and predicted actions.

Ownership adds another layer. In many systems, the organization collecting the data claims control over it, regardless of who it represents. But that assumption is increasingly being challenged—by privacy advocates, by regulators, and by users themselves. Should a hospital own the digital twin of your heart? Should a company own the behavioral model of its employees? Should a city own the movement data of its citizens?

There's no easy answer, but there's a growing expectation that data should at least be co-owned. Individuals should have access to their digital profiles. They should be able to see what's collected, make corrections, request deletion, or limit how their data is used. This isn't about obstructing innovation—it's about aligning it with fairness.

And it's not just a legal or ethical issue—it's a strategic one. Companies that proactively give users control over their data will build stronger relationships. They'll attract better talent, more loyal customers, and fewer headaches from regulators. They'll also design better systems—because when people trust the process, they're more willing to participate fully and honestly, enriching the very data the system depends on.

Consent also needs to be ongoing, not one-time. People's expectations change. Their roles evolve. What someone was comfortable sharing during onboarding might feel invasive a year later. The ability to pause, adjust, or withdraw consent should be built into digital twin platforms by design, not tacked on later in response to backlash.

This is especially important when data is shared across systems or used to train algorithms. Consent for one purpose doesn't imply consent for all. A user might be fine with their data helping to improve a product but completely opposed to it being sold to third parties or used for unrelated research. Respecting those boundaries isn't just good ethics—it's good engineering.

There's also the question of monetization. If a company profits from a digital twin built largely from user-generated data, does the user deserve a share? Should there be compensation models, even if small, for contributing to large-scale behavioral or environmental insights? It's a question that's gaining traction, especially in industries where personal data drives product value—healthcare, retail, mobility.

At its core, this all comes down to agency. People don't just want to be subjects in someone else's model. They want to be participants—with rights, visibility, and a sense of control over how they're represented. Digital twins, when done right, can support that agency. They can provide personalized services, enhance experiences, and even save lives. But they have to be built on foundations of respect and transparency.

Otherwise, the backlash will come—not just from regulators, but from the very people these systems are supposed to serve.

True innovation isn't just about what technology makes possible. It's about what people are willing to support, and that starts with giving them a voice in how their data shapes the world around them.

Safety in Autonomous and AI-Driven Systems

The moment a system begins making decisions without human input, the stakes change. Whether it's an autonomous vehicle navigating city streets, a robot handling fragile materials on a factory floor, or a predictive model rerouting foot traffic in real time, safety becomes more than a checklist—it becomes a moving target. Digital twins play a critical role in shaping how these systems learn, respond, and evolve. But with that power comes a new kind of responsibility, one that blends engineering, ethics, and real-world risk.

At the core of autonomy is trust in machine judgment. We assume that the AI will do what it's supposed to do. That it will make the right call, adapt to the unexpected, and avoid harm. But how do we know? The answer, increasingly, lies in simulation—specifically, the kind that digital twins make possible. Virtual environments allow autonomous systems to train on edge cases, test thousands of scenarios, and build a kind of experience before they ever enter the real world. That's the good news.

The challenge is that even the most sophisticated digital twin is still a model—a representation, not reality. And when the model is wrong, or incomplete, or too optimistic, autonomous systems can fail in ways that are fast, unpredictable, and dangerous. It doesn't take a catastrophic crash to create doubt. All it takes is one misread signal, one corner case the model didn't anticipate, and suddenly people question whether the system was ever safe to begin with.

This is where transparency becomes non-negotiable. If a digital twin powers an AI that controls something in the physical world, there needs to be a clear understanding of how that twin is constructed, maintained, and validated. What data is it pulling from? How often is it updated? What are its blind spots? And perhaps most importantly—what is the process when the system gets something wrong?

Because it will. Every AI system makes mistakes. The question isn't how to eliminate error altogether—that's impossible. The real question is how quickly the system can detect, correct, and learn from its errors without causing harm. That requires more than just high-fidelity modeling. It demands fail-safes, override mechanisms, and human-in-the-loop protocols that keep control within reach when needed.

In environments like manufacturing or healthcare, this balance is especially sensitive. A robot that misplaces a part on an assembly line can create costly delays. A robot-assisted surgery system that misinterprets anatomical data can have far more serious consequences.

The role of the digital twin here is twofold: first, to act as a sandbox where systems can be tested under stress, and second, to continuously monitor real-time operations for deviations that suggest risk.

But even with those safeguards, the deployment of AI-driven systems requires a mindset shift. It's not just about performance metrics. It's about responsibility. Who's accountable when an autonomous system makes a harmful decision based on flawed inputs from its digital twin? The manufacturer? The software developer? The organization deploying it?

These are the kinds of questions regulators are starting to ask. And while laws are still catching up, public opinion isn't waiting. People expect that if a machine is going to act independently—especially in spaces where safety is on the line—someone should be held accountable when things go wrong.

It's also worth noting that safety isn't just physical. In many AI-driven systems, especially those powered by behavioral or biometric data, the danger lies in the assumptions the model makes. If a predictive system assumes someone is likely to act a certain way, and takes action based on that assumption, it can lead to discrimination, exclusion, or denial of service. That kind of harm is quieter than a malfunctioning robot, but no less real.

The way to prevent these issues is not by slowing down innovation, but by making safety integral to the innovation process. That means bringing ethicists, safety engineers, and diverse user groups into the design phase. It means stress-testing models against bias, not just performance. It means acknowledging uncertainty and building systems that can fail gracefully rather than catastrophically.

Digital twins are uniquely positioned to support this because they give us a testing ground that's rich, flexible, and risk-free. But only if we use them that way. Rushing deployment to market without sufficient simulation time, skipping edge case analysis, or ignoring known model limitations—these are choices, not accidents. And they're the kind of choices that erode confidence in autonomous systems long-term.

Safety in AI isn't a feature. It's a foundation. And in the world of digital twins, it's the invisible layer that supports everything else. No amount of efficiency or cost savings will make up for systems that people don't feel safe using or being around. The moment that trust breaks, adoption stalls—and the promise of the technology is lost.

This is why the smartest companies are already shifting their thinking. They're not just asking, "Can we make this autonomous?" They're asking, "Can we make this safe, reliable, and trustworthy at scale?" The difference might seem subtle, but it's the difference between something that impresses in a demo and something that earns its place in the real world.

Bias, Error Margins, and Fail-Safes

Every system has blind spots. Every model carries assumptions. The danger comes when we forget that—or worse, pretend it isn't true. In the world of digital twins, where real-world decisions are increasingly driven by virtual representations, the consequences of bias and error can ripple far beyond the screen.

Bias doesn't always look like prejudice. Sometimes, it's baked into the data—what's collected, who it's collected from, and how it's labeled. Other times, it sneaks in through the design of the model itself. A logistics twin trained only on urban traffic data might perform brilliantly in New York but fail in Nairobi. A predictive maintenance system built with data from high-end machinery might overestimate what older equipment can handle. None of this is intentional, but it still skews results.

And when digital twins feed into autonomous or semi-autonomous systems—whether it's in manufacturing, urban planning, or healthcare—that skew has impact. It shapes decisions. It affects safety, equity, and efficiency. Left unchecked, it reinforces inequality, fuels mistrust, and limits the technology's usefulness.

This is why bias isn't just a fairness issue. It's a performance issue. A twin that only works well under ideal conditions isn't a reliable twin. Real-world environments are messy, diverse, and full of edge cases. Systems that can't navigate that complexity are fragile by default.

Error margins are another layer of this equation. No model is perfect. No simulation captures every variable. Digital twins, even at their most sophisticated, are still approximations. They work best when those approximations are known, documented, and built into the system's logic. But too often, error margins are treated as minor footnotes—or ignored entirely.

What's the acceptable range of inaccuracy for a smart grid's energy model? How much lag is tolerable in a real-time hospital monitoring twin? What level of prediction confidence justifies action in an AI-driven vehicle fleet? These aren't academic questions. They're operational ones. And without clear answers, systems can be overtrusted or underused—both of which create risk.

Fail-safes are the guardrails. They're what catch problems when bias slips through or an error margin gets breached. And they're just as important as the models themselves. A fail-safe might be a human override button, a secondary sensor system, or even an alert mechanism that flags anomalies for manual review. It's the difference between a twin that assumes it's right and one that checks itself when things start going sideways.

Designing effective fail-safes means understanding where and how systems are most likely to fail. It means asking hard questions: What happens if the data feed goes dark? What if the input gets corrupted? What if the output triggers something dangerous, and no one's around to stop it?

In high-stakes environments—say, aerospace or intensive care units—these questions are life-or-death. But even in less critical settings, poor assumptions can cascade. An inaccurate forecast in a supply chain twin can result in lost revenue, missed deadlines, or inventory waste. A faulty pedestrian recognition model in a smart city system could lead to policy decisions that harm vulnerable communities.

It's not enough to hope systems work as intended. We need to design for when they don't.

One way to do that is by building diversity into the data itself. Diverse inputs reduce blind spots. They help models generalize better and behave more reliably across different populations, environments, and use cases. Another strategy is stress testing—intentionally pushing the twin to its limits to see where it cracks. This kind of pre-failure exploration is essential. It doesn't just reveal weaknesses—it teaches teams how to respond to them.

But the most powerful fail-safe of all might be humility. A willingness to acknowledge uncertainty, to document known limitations, and to involve people in the loop where judgment matters most. Autonomous systems don't need to replace humans. They need to work alongside them—especially when outcomes are uncertain or data is incomplete.

The companies getting this right aren't the ones racing toward full automation at all costs. They're the ones designing systems that can pause, ask for help, and learn over time. That humility is what makes a digital twin trustworthy—not just accurate.

And when something does go wrong—and eventually it will—what matters most is how the system reacts. Can it contain the failure? Can it recover gracefully? Can it log what happened and learn from it? A twin that collapses under pressure is just a shiny simulation. A twin that adapts and improves becomes an asset with long-term value.

In the end, bias, error margins, and fail-safes aren't technical side issues. They're core to the mission of building systems people can depend on. They're not just about doing things right—they're about doing the right things, in a world that's never as clean or predictable as a data model makes it seem.

Regulatory Landscape Across Industries

The rules are catching up, but slowly. As digital twins stretch across industries—from manufacturing to medicine, smart cities to retail—governments and regulatory bodies are still figuring out how to keep pace. In many cases, the technology is out ahead of the law, creating gray zones where businesses move fast and regulators scramble to define the lines after the fact. That gap brings opportunity, but also risk, especially when lives, privacy, and power dynamics are involved.

Regulation isn't one-size-fits-all. What's acceptable in logistics might raise red flags in healthcare. A digital twin that tracks movement patterns in a warehouse is treated very differently from one modeling a patient's heart or a citizen's behavior in a public space. The context changes everything. And while certain principles—like consent, safety, and accountability—cut across all domains, the specifics vary dramatically.

In the healthcare space, regulation is already intense, as it should be. Devices and systems that use patient data must comply with strict frameworks like HIPAA in the United States or GDPR in the European Union when sensitive health data is involved. If a digital twin is being used to simulate a surgical procedure, monitor vitals in real time, or forecast disease risk based on behavioral data, it falls under the umbrella of medical devices in many jurisdictions. That means extensive documentation, transparency about data use, rigorous validation, and in some cases, certification from national health authorities.

On the other end of the spectrum, sectors like retail or manufacturing have historically operated with fewer data governance rules—at least until recently. But that's changing fast. As digital twins start collecting more behavioral, biometric, and environmental data—often through AI—the lines begin to blur. What counts as personally identifiable information? How long can it be stored? Who's responsible for its protection when third-party vendors and cloud platforms are involved?

In Europe, GDPR has set a global tone. It emphasizes consent, data minimization, and the right to be forgotten—principles that are forcing companies to rethink how their digital twin ecosystems are structured. But even GDPR leaves room for interpretation, especially when it comes to real-time systems and emerging use cases that didn't exist when the law was written. And in the U.S., the regulatory landscape is even more fragmented. Privacy laws vary state by state. There's no single federal law governing how digital twin data can or should be used, which puts the burden on companies to navigate a patchwork of expectations.

Meanwhile, in places like China or Singapore, regulatory frameworks are often more centralized but also more permissive when aligned with national goals. In these countries, large-scale digital twin projects—like smart cities or public health platforms—move forward with strong government backing and fewer barriers to data integration. That speed can drive innovation, but it also raises concerns about surveillance and individual rights, especially when citizens don't have a say in how their digital presence is used or stored.

What we're seeing is a global divergence. Some regions are leaning hard into privacy and user rights. Others are prioritizing innovation and efficiency. For companies operating across borders, this creates complexity—not just legal complexity, but ethical tension. A system that's fully compliant in one country might be considered invasive in another. And as consumers and employees become more aware of their data rights, businesses are being forced to rise to the highest standard, not just the lowest legal threshold.

There's also the question of liability. When a digital twin system causes harm—whether through a predictive failure, a breach of privacy, or a biased decision—who's held responsible? Is it the organization that deployed the system? The software developer? The data provider? Right now, many of those lines are unclear. And in the absence of regulation, legal precedent becomes the fallback—often after the damage is done.

That's why some forward-looking industries are taking the initiative to self-regulate. Aerospace and automotive manufacturers, for instance, have been building internal standards for simulation accuracy, data security, and system redundancy long before public agencies intervened. These industries understand that when trust breaks—whether with regulators or the public—the fallout is expensive and hard to repair.

Technology companies building digital twin platforms are also starting to publish ethical frameworks, audit logs, and transparency reports to demonstrate accountability before it's legally required. They know that regulation is coming—and in some cases, they'd rather shape it than be blindsided by it.

Still, voluntary guidelines only go so far. At some point, clear and enforceable rules become necessary—not just to protect users, but to create a level playing field. When everyone's held to the same baseline of responsibility, innovation can move faster without cutting corners.

The future of regulation won't be about restricting digital twins—it'll be about making them safer, more equitable, and more trusted. That means laws that are nuanced enough to reflect different use cases, agile enough to evolve with the tech, and strong enough to hold bad actors accountable.

Until then, the smartest path forward is caution paired with clarity. If a company is unsure how their digital twin initiative fits into the legal framework, the answer isn't to wait and see. It's to seek guidance, set internal standards, and build as if regulation already exists.

Because soon, it will.

It's not enough to build what's possible. What matters is building what's responsible. The long-term value of digital twins will hinge not just on their technical precision, but on how transparently they're used, how fairly they treat data, and how thoughtfully they account for human lives behind the models. Companies that take these questions seriously won't just avoid risk—they'll build trust, drive adoption, and shape the future of digital innovation on solid ground.

Chapter 15

What's Next? Digital Twins and Intelligent Environments

The boundary between physical and digital is starting to blur—not just in how we model reality, but in how we interact with it. Digital twins are no longer passive reflections of the world; they're beginning to influence it in real time, making decisions, adapting environments, and co-creating outcomes with human input. What began as a tool for monitoring and simulation is quickly evolving into something more dynamic: a foundation for intelligent environments where digital systems don't just observe—they participate.

Beyond Mirroring: Predictive and Autonomous Environments

At first, digital twins were mirrors. They reflected the world with accuracy and clarity, offering a way to see

314

what was happening in real time. That alone was revolutionary—having a live replica of a factory, city grid, or human body changed how businesses operated, how doctors diagnosed, and how city planners designed. But mirroring is just the beginning. The real shift is what happens when these digital twins start to act.

Predictive environments are the next evolution. These are systems that don't just observe current conditions—they anticipate what's coming next. A smart building, for example, might use data from occupancy patterns, weather forecasts, and energy prices to adjust HVAC usage before anyone arrives. A digital twin of a power grid might shift loads preemptively based on usage trends and upcoming events. These environments rely on patterns, probability, and speed—using past behavior to get ahead of future need.

Prediction in this context isn't just a nice feature. It's a survival trait. When systems can't keep up with the pace of real-world change, they fall behind. Predictive environments keep operations not just stable, but agile. They can catch bottlenecks before they form, prevent breakdowns before they happen, and reroute resources before shortages hit. That foresight changes the equation from reactive to proactive. And in high-stakes sectors like transportation, logistics, or healthcare, that shift can be the difference between smooth operation and crisis.

But even that is still tethered to human oversight. What happens when the environment begins to act on its own?

Autonomous environments take the concept further. They're not just predictive—they're responsive. They adjust themselves based on what the digital twin sees, learns, and determines. A warehouse might reorganize itself overnight based on inventory flow. A public transit system might reroute buses and trains dynamically, based on real-time foot traffic. An autonomous twin of a manufacturing plant could not only flag a machine as overheating—it could schedule a repair, reroute production, and notify the supply chain team, all without waiting for human input.

This is where digital twins begin to merge with AI in a deeper way. The twin provides the situational awareness—the what, where, when, and sometimes why. The AI brings the decision logic, trained on past outcomes and optimized for performance, safety, or cost. Together, they form environments that adapt in real time, learn over time, and eventually start to operate with a kind of agency.

And while that might sound futuristic, it's already happening. Some airports are experimenting with digital twins that optimize terminal flows dynamically—adjusting escalator directions, queue management systems, and gate assignments based on the movement of thousands of people. Smart traffic systems in urban environments are using predictive models to adjust traffic light timing without human intervention. These are real-world examples of autonomous environments in action—subtle, quiet, but deeply transformative.

Of course, the leap from predictive to autonomous comes with new challenges. When the system acts on its own, accountability becomes a major concern. Who's responsible if the AI makes the wrong call? What guardrails exist to stop cascading errors? How do you ensure the environment doesn't optimize for the wrong thing—like speed over safety, or efficiency over fairness?

Designing autonomous environments requires more than just great tech. It requires values. What matters in this space? What principles guide the way decisions are made? Those values need to be embedded at the architecture level, not layered on later. And they need to be dynamic, able to evolve as conditions, stakeholders, and goals change.

Another tension arises around visibility. In predictive systems, humans are still part of the loop—they see what's forecasted and can intervene. In autonomous systems, much of the work happens invisibly. That makes transparency a serious issue. People don't trust what they don't understand. If a factory floor is suddenly rearranged by an AI, workers need to know why. If a traffic system starts prioritizing certain routes over others, citizens deserve a rationale.

This is why the shift from mirroring to acting needs to be paired with storytelling. Not in the marketing sense, but in the way systems explain themselves. Can the twin show how it reached a decision? Can it surface the variables, assumptions, and trade-offs involved? This kind of explainability isn't just a nice-to-have—it's essential for adoption. Especially in environments where people's safety, privacy, or daily experience is on the line.

There's also a cultural layer. Predictive and autonomous environments don't just change how systems run—they change how people relate to those systems. In some workplaces, automation is seen as a threat. In others, it's a relief. The difference often comes down to how the transition is handled. Was the shift transparent? Were workers involved in shaping the rules? Do people feel the system works with them, or around them?

When digital twins cross into autonomy, human-machine relationships become critical. People need to know the environment sees them, understands them, and adapts to them—not just the other way around. That's where trust is built. And that's what will determine whether these intelligent environments are embraced or resisted.

What's exciting is that we're no longer imagining this future. We're building it. One twin, one space, one system at a time. The shift from mirroring to acting is underway. It's already redefining what environments can do—and what we expect from them.

The real question now isn't whether our spaces will think and respond. It's whether we'll design them to think clearly, respond fairly, and act in ways we can live with.

Digital Twins as Inputs for Generative Design

Design used to be a top-down process. A team would gather requirements, sketch ideas, run simulations, and inch their way toward a solution. It was a cycle of trial, refinement, and guesswork—human-led, tool-assisted. But now that digital twins can feed real-time, high-resolution data into the process, that model is changing. Design is becoming dynamic, adaptive, and in some cases, generative.

Generative design flips the traditional approach. Instead of humans drafting a concept and testing it, the system generates multiple solutions based on input parameters, performance goals, and constraints. It doesn't replace the designer—it becomes a partner in the creative process, offering options that a human team might never consider on their own. And digital twins make this possible by providing the most accurate, current, and context-rich inputs the system could ask for.

The power of generative design lies in how it handles complexity. A single building might need to balance energy efficiency, occupant comfort, daylight exposure, airflow, and cost. With traditional tools, that balance is approached through compromise and iteration. With a digital twin feeding live data into a generative engine, the system can explore thousands—or millions—of possible configurations, all grounded in real-world conditions.

For example, an architect working on a new office building could plug in the digital twin of an existing structure, complete with environmental data, usage patterns, and energy performance metrics. The generative system then uses that information to propose design variations that outperform the original on key metrics—say, 20% lower energy use, or improved airflow in high-traffic zones. The architect still makes the final call, but now they're making it with more options and better data.

It doesn't stop at buildings. In manufacturing, digital twins of machines and materials can inform generative designs for products that are lighter, stronger, or more efficient to produce. Aerospace companies are already using this approach to create parts that look almost alien—organic forms shaped not by human intuition but by optimization algorithms trained on twin-derived insights. These parts often perform better and cost less, because the system found performance curves humans wouldn't have thought to explore.

Urban planning is another frontier. City twins that model pedestrian flow, energy usage, and weather patterns can drive the generative design of public spaces, transit systems, or entire neighborhoods. Instead of designing for static assumptions, planners can design for how people actually move and interact in real-time environments. That kind of responsiveness changes everything—from how parks are laid out to how emergency routes are planned.

The same is starting to happen in logistics, healthcare, even interface design. As twins become more contextual and behavior-aware, they enable generative systems to propose better layouts, workflows, and experiences—faster than human teams ever could. But the shift here isn't just technical. It's philosophical.

We're moving from design as control to design as collaboration—with systems that can learn, propose, and adapt alongside us. That kind of co-creation has its own challenges. One is knowing when to trust the system. Generative outputs aren't always perfect, and not every surprising solution is a good one. There needs to be a layer of interpretation, critique, and values-driven oversight. In other words, the human role doesn't disappear—it evolves.

There's also the issue of explainability. If a system generates a design, stakeholders need to understand why that solution emerged. What trade-offs were made? What data influenced it? If a generative tool proposes a hospital layout that saves money but reduces visibility from nurses' stations to patient rooms, that choice needs to be surfaced—not buried under layers of math. Digital twins can help with that too, offering not just inputs but interpretive layers that bring transparency to the design logic.

Generative design isn't about handing over the reins. It's about giving teams more visibility into what's possible—beyond their assumptions, constraints, and cognitive bandwidth. With digital twins feeding in real-world data, those possibilities become more grounded and more relevant. The system doesn't just imagine new futures—it bases them on actual conditions, real constraints, and live performance feedback.

And that means the designs aren't just better on paper—they're more resilient in the real world. When conditions shift, digital twins can inform design updates in real time. A layout that worked in spring might need to change in winter. A logistics flow that's optimal during low demand could break under a holiday rush. With twins integrated into generative systems, those shifts become part of the design loop—not afterthoughts, but live variables.

What's emerging is a world where design is no longer static. It's iterative, intelligent, and context-aware. Teams aren't starting from scratch—they're starting from insight. And as digital twins grow more detailed, more embedded, and more personalized, the generative systems they fuel will create designs that aren't just high-performing—they're alive.

This isn't about making machines more creative. It's about giving humans better tools to imagine what comes next—and the feedback loops to make sure it works when it gets there.

Real-Time, Closed-Loop Decision-Making

In most organizations, decisions happen in stages. Something occurs, data is collected, a report is run, someone analyzes it, and eventually, a decision is made. By the time action is taken, the moment may have already passed. Digital twins are beginning to dismantle that timeline. They're creating environments where observation, analysis, and action happen in the same breath—what's often called closed-loop decision-making.

A closed loop means the system doesn't just monitor reality—it acts on it, and then monitors the outcome of that action to inform the next move. It's an ongoing feedback cycle, powered by real-time data and intelligent logic, where the gap between insight and execution disappears. This model shifts decision-making from periodic and reactive to continuous and adaptive. And when done well, it creates systems that feel alive—constantly learning, refining, and improving.

Imagine a logistics hub where sensors track every movement of goods, personnel, and vehicles. A digital twin processes those inputs instantly and flags a potential delay due to a misrouted package. Instead of waiting for a supervisor to read a report, the system autonomously adjusts the routing, updates estimated delivery times, alerts stakeholders, and monitors the result. If the change solves the problem, it's logged as a new standard. If not, the system tries again. That's closed-loop logic in action.

The power of this approach lies in its immediacy. When feedback loops are tight, systems can course-correct before issues escalate. A slight change in vibration on a factory motor might trigger predictive maintenance before a breakdown. A subtle shift in temperature inside a cold-storage unit might adjust airflow to prevent spoilage. In all these cases, the digital twin isn't just a passive observer. It's a decision node in the system—a place where action starts.

Real-time, closed-loop decision-making isn't just about speed. It's about precision. Decisions are no longer based on broad assumptions or stale reports—they're based on up-to-the-second realities. That means fewer overcorrections, less guesswork, and smarter resource use. It also opens the door to optimization at a level that humans alone can't achieve. In a city traffic system, for instance, a digital twin might adjust light patterns across dozens of intersections simultaneously, balancing flow in a way no human dispatcher could manage in real time.

But the leap to closed-loop systems requires trust—both in the data and in the logic driving the responses. If the twin is working off outdated or incomplete data, the whole loop breaks. If the decision-making layer is poorly designed, it could trigger harmful or unnecessary actions. That's why these systems must be built with rigorous validation, clear parameters, and mechanisms for human override.

It also means thinking carefully about where autonomy makes sense and where human judgment should remain in the loop. Not every process benefits from full automation. In healthcare, for example, a twin might detect anomalies in patient vitals and suggest interventions—but it should never replace the clinician's decision-making. Instead, it becomes a guide, a second set of eyes, constantly analyzing patterns and providing context.

Closed-loop systems also raise the bar for accountability. If a decision is made autonomously and leads to a bad outcome, who's responsible? The software vendor? The team that deployed the twin? The organization that approved the logic? These are questions every company needs to answer before pushing the "auto" button. And they need to be asked not just from a liability standpoint, but from a trust standpoint. Because people won't engage with systems they feel powerless to question or correct.

Another key consideration is explainability. In a closed-loop system, where actions happen quickly and often invisibly, it's easy for users to feel out of the loop. That's dangerous. Every action the system takes should come with a traceable rationale—a way to audit why the twin recommended this route, not that one; why it triggered this alert, not another. Without that visibility, even high-performing systems will be met with skepticism or pushback.

There's also a learning layer to consider. In the best closed-loop environments, the system doesn't just respond—it evolves. Each loop teaches the twin something. It refines predictions, sharpens thresholds, and adjusts the weight it gives to different inputs. Over time, the environment gets smarter—not just in the AI sense, but in its ability to align with human needs, operational goals, and changing contexts.

In many ways, closed-loop decision-making brings digital twins full circle. They start by reflecting reality, but they end by reshaping it—continuously, intelligently, and often invisibly. The spaces and systems around us start to adapt without being told, based on patterns they recognize and outcomes they learn from. And that opens up new territory, not just for optimization, but for real transformation.

We're already seeing this shift in industries that need to move fast—aviation, manufacturing, energy. But it's spreading quickly. Schools, hospitals, even individual homes are beginning to adopt systems that react and adapt on the fly. Over time, these loops will become as common as dashboards are today. The question isn't whether we'll use them, but how we'll shape the logic behind them.

Because once the system begins to act, the philosophy behind the code becomes policy. And that's where the real decisions are made.

Human-AI Collaboration in Spatial Environments

When digital twins first entered the scene, they were seen as tools—technological assistants that helped humans make better decisions. But as these systems become more intelligent, more aware, and more autonomous, the relationship between humans and machines is shifting. We're moving from tools to teammates. From assistance to collaboration. Nowhere is that more visible than in spatial environments—places where people and AI physically share space, respond to each other, and influence one another in real time.

In a factory, this might look like robots working side by side with human technicians. The digital twin of the environment tracks machine health, workflow patterns, and safety zones. It updates in real time and feeds that information to both the AI systems controlling the machines and the people supervising them. The result? A kind of co-awareness—each side adapting based on what the other is doing. The AI slows down when a human enters a certain zone. The worker trusts that they won't be surprised by a sudden movement. It's choreography, not just computation.

In a hospital, this collaboration takes on a more supportive form. Digital twins of patient rooms track environmental conditions, staff movement, and medical equipment usage. AI interprets those patterns, flagging inefficiencies or risks. But instead of making decisions in isolation, the system surfaces recommendations—like adjusting nurse shift patterns or suggesting equipment reallocation—and leaves the judgment to human teams. The AI becomes a partner in situational awareness, not a replacement for professional intuition.

What makes these environments so powerful is the real-time feedback loop between people and systems. Spatial digital twins give both sides the ability to "see" what's happening: humans get contextual overlays, predictive alerts, or visual cues through AR interfaces, while AI systems track human behavior as part of the data stream. The line between user and system begins to blur. People aren't just operating the environment—they're part of it.

This collaboration works best when each side knows what the other is good at. AI is fast, consistent, and tireless. Humans are nuanced, empathetic, and flexible. The most effective systems don't try to flatten those differences—they build around them. A warehouse picker might wear smart glasses powered by a spatial twin, guiding them through the most efficient route while accounting for live changes in inventory or aisle congestion. But the worker can override the suggestion when they spot an issue the AI missed—maybe a box that's fallen or a label that's been swapped. Each action feeds back into the system, improving the next recommendation.

It's this interplay—machine proposes, human adapts, system learns—that defines next-generation environments. But it only works if the systems are designed to be collaborative from the start. Too many AI implementations treat human input as noise to be reduced, not a signal to be integrated. In spatial settings, that approach fails. These environments are dynamic, unpredictable, and full of edge cases. Human presence isn't a flaw—it's a feature.

Designing for collaboration also means paying close attention to interfaces. How do people receive input from the system? How do they give feedback? Is it visual, tactile, voice-based, gesture-based? Do workers feel empowered or constrained? Does the technology support their workflow, or interrupt it? These questions don't just affect adoption—they shape the effectiveness of the system itself.

Trust is another pillar. People are more likely to rely on AI systems that are transparent, consistent, and accountable. That means showing not just what the system is doing, but why. It means allowing room for disagreement, feedback, and even refusal. If a recommendation doesn't make sense, the person using it should feel confident in pushing back. And the system should be designed to learn from that input, not ignore it.

The emotional layer of collaboration matters, too. People bring judgment, stress, intuition—and sometimes, fatigue. AI systems need to be sensitive to that. A well-designed spatial twin might notice when a team is overloaded and automatically reduce nonessential alerts. Or it might shift workload distribution across a building based on movement patterns, giving breathing room to areas that are congested. These aren't just efficiency improvements. They're signals of respect—design choices that treat people as partners, not cogs.

At a broader level, spatial collaboration invites us to rethink leadership and decision-making. In an environment where AI systems surface insights and suggestions constantly, who sets the priorities? Who gets the final say? And how do you balance data-driven logic with human experience? These aren't just technical challenges—they're cultural ones. Teams need to evolve, too. Managers need to understand not just what the system can do, but when to lean on it—and when to step in.

This kind of collaboration won't look the same everywhere. In a high-speed logistics center, the system might drive 90% of the decisions, with humans stepping in for anomalies. In a hospital, it might be flipped—AI offers suggestions, but the human clinician holds the reins. The key is flexibility. Systems need to understand the roles they're playing, and those roles need to adapt over time as trust, experience, and context evolve.

Ultimately, human-AI collaboration in spatial environments isn't about making the human obsolete. It's about making both sides better. Smarter spaces are only truly intelligent when they account for the intelligence inside them—the people. And the most powerful digital twins won't just see and simulate—they'll listen, learn, and co-create.

This is the future of work, care, movement, and interaction. Not humans versus machines. Not humans controlled by machines. But humans with machines—working together in environments that are built to respond, respect, and evolve.

The Future of Digital Twins in Home, Work, and Public Spaces & Long-Term Vision: Sustainable, Self-Optimizing Systems

We often think of digital twins as industrial tools, confined to factories, infrastructure, or enterprise-scale systems. But they're already beginning to step into more personal, more intimate spaces—our homes, our workplaces, the cities we move through every day. As they become smaller, smarter, and more integrated, digital twins are transitioning from specialized software to the invisible architecture of daily life.

At home, it starts with simple things. A thermostat that knows your habits, a fridge that tracks expiration dates, a mirror that reminds you to hydrate. But beneath these conveniences is a deeper shift. Each of these systems builds a model—not just of your preferences, but of your rhythms, your patterns, even your wellbeing. Over time, these micro-twins connect, creating a holistic view of your living space as a responsive environment. One that anticipates, adapts, and learns—not just from your inputs, but from your behavior.

In workplaces, the role of digital twins is growing more sophisticated. Offices that once operated on fixed schedules and static floor plans are being replaced with fluid spaces shaped by live occupancy data, energy loads, and task-based collaboration. A meeting room isn't just a room—it's a node in a larger network of space usage, environmental controls, and employee wellbeing. Sensors, wearables, and ambient data feeds feed into twins that help employers understand how space supports productivity—or stifles it. And in hybrid or remote-first work cultures, digital twins help bridge the physical and digital divide, ensuring remote environments are just as visible, functional, and safe as in-office ones.

Then there are public spaces—the streets, parks, transit systems, and infrastructure that underpin urban life. City-scale digital twins are already making decisions that affect millions of people: how traffic is routed, how waste is managed, how air quality is monitored. These systems are becoming more democratic and more personal. Citizens interact with them through mobile apps, sensors in public transit, or even through their energy usage at home. Every touchpoint becomes part of a larger picture—a living model of the city that evolves with every movement, transaction, and choice.

As these environments grow smarter, so does their potential to become not just adaptive, but sustainable in the truest sense. That's where the long-term vision begins to take shape. Digital twins aren't just about efficiency or convenience anymore—they're about systems that can take care of themselves. Environments that respond to stressors before we notice them. Buildings that reduce their own carbon footprints. Communities that optimize resource use in real time, dynamically balancing energy, transportation, and access without needing constant human oversight.

A sustainable, self-optimizing system is one that doesn't wait for something to break. It predicts. It rebalances. It learns from the past and adjusts for the future. It doesn't just save energy—it allocates it based on changing demand, climate conditions, and social impact. It doesn't just plan transportation—it redesigns routes based on real-time patterns and long-term health outcomes. These aren't distant goals. They're already being prototyped in districts, campuses, and forward-looking cities around the world.

But sustainability isn't just about efficiency. It's also about resilience. A truly optimized system doesn't crumble under stress—it adapts. A digital twin of a power grid might reroute energy during a blackout to preserve critical systems. A twin of a food distribution network might adjust sourcing during a supply chain shock. These systems don't just help us build stronger infrastructure—they help us prepare for the unexpected.

And they open up space for something else: equity. Because when systems become more intelligent, they can be taught to prioritize not just profit or performance, but access, fairness, and wellbeing. A twin of a transit network can be trained to reduce commute times for underserved communities. A city twin can simulate different zoning policies to explore who gains and who's left out. Optimization becomes a tool not just for growth, but for justice—if we build it that way.

This future won't arrive all at once. It will come through choices—small, steady decisions made by companies, governments, communities, and individuals. Choosing systems that listen, that adapt, that respect the people they serve. Choosing transparency over convenience. Collaboration over control. Designing not just for what works, but for what matters.

We're entering an era where environments will no longer be static. They will learn us. Respond to us. And in some cases, challenge us to rethink what we need, what we value, and how we want to live. That kind of power demands care. And imagination. And a deep sense of responsibility.

Digital twins will not be the future. The choices we make with them will be.

The path ahead isn't just about sharper models or faster data. It's about shifting how we think about space, behavior, and collaboration. Digital twins are becoming part of the environment itself—embedded in infrastructure, products, even our homes and cities. They will shape how we work, move, heal, and live. But this future doesn't arrive fully formed. It's built—intentionally, incrementally, and with care.

The question now is no longer if digital twins will transform our world—but how. And whether we'll shape them with clarity, purpose, and responsibility—or let them shape us without it.

Appendices

As digital twins move from cutting-edge to commonplace, the need for clarity grows. Whether you're new to the space or building out your second implementation, having a shared language, a few trusted tools, and a sense of what's out there can make the difference between a stalled pilot and a successful rollout. This appendix brings together key terms, file formats, frameworks, and resources to keep you grounded as the field continues to expand.

Glossary of Terms

Digital twin technology pulls from multiple disciplines—engineering, data science, AI, spatial computing—which means the vocabulary can get dense, fast. Here are some foundational terms that come up frequently:

- Pose: Refers to the position and orientation of an object or person in space. It's not just where something is, but how it's facing, angled, or moving. Used heavily in robotics, AR/VR, and human modeling.

- Bounding Box: A virtual rectangle or cube that frames an object in 2D or 3D space. Bounding boxes are essential for object detection, collision avoidance, and defining spatial limits within a scene.
- Segmentation: The process of dividing an image or environment into parts, labeling each region according to what it represents (e.g., floor, human, wall, equipment). This enables systems to understand context and interact more precisely with their surroundings.
- Scene Graph: A hierarchical structure used to organize the spatial relationships and rendering order of objects in a digital environment. Common in gaming, simulation, and 3D modeling.
- Sensor Fusion: The combining of data from multiple sensor sources (e.g., cameras, LIDAR, accelerometers) to build a more accurate and comprehensive picture of the physical world.
- Latency: The delay between an input being received and a response being generated. Low-latency systems are critical for real-time digital twins.
- Fidelity: Describes how closely a digital twin replicates the physical object or environment it represents—higher fidelity means more detail, more accuracy, and often more data processing.

Industry Standards and File Formats

As the digital twin space matures, standardization is becoming essential. Without shared formats, collaboration across platforms or organizations becomes difficult. Here are a few of the most widely used and emerging standards:

- USD (Universal Scene Description): Originally developed by Pixar, USD is designed to handle complex 3D environments and has become a foundational format for spatial computing and digital twin modeling. Its layered structure allows for scalable, collaborative workflows.
- GLTF (GL Transmission Format): Often described as the "JPEG of 3D," GLTF is optimized for the efficient transmission and rendering of 3D scenes and models. It's widely used in web-based and mobile applications.
- FBX and OBJ: Legacy 3D file formats still in use, particularly in animation and CAD-heavy workflows. They're often converted to more modern formats like GLTF or USD for real-time applications.
- MQTT and OPC UA: Communication protocols used for connecting industrial systems and IoT devices. These enable different components of a digital twin ecosystem—sensors, edge devices,

analytics engines—to talk to each other reliably and securely.

- ROS (Robot Operating System): An open-source framework often used in robotics that supports sensor integration, environment mapping, and real-time data sharing—key components in digital twin development.

Toolkits and Frameworks

You don't need to build a digital twin platform from scratch. Several robust tools and ecosystems exist to accelerate development, improve accuracy, and support scalability. Here are some of the most impactful:

- Intel Scenescape: A spatial intelligence platform built to create context-aware environments by combining real-time sensor data, AI processing, and spatial mapping. Ideal for use cases where understanding physical space is critical—retail, smart buildings, autonomous systems.
- Mevea: Specializes in high-fidelity physics-based simulations, particularly in industrial and engineering contexts. Their digital twin solutions are used for virtual prototyping, operator training, and predictive maintenance, offering a "physics-first" approach that tightly mirrors real-world conditions.

- USD Framework (Pixar/NVIDIA Omniverse): Beyond file formatting, USD is also the backbone of platforms like NVIDIA Omniverse, which support real-time collaboration and simulation across teams and industries. These environments are ideal for complex, multi-stakeholder digital twin projects.
- Unity and Unreal Engine: While traditionally used in gaming, both engines are now widely adopted in digital twin development for their high-quality rendering, flexible APIs, and support for real-time interaction. They are especially useful in AR/VR environments and spatial simulations.
- AWS IoT TwinMaker / Microsoft Azure Digital Twins / Siemens Xcelerator: These cloud-based platforms provide scalable infrastructure for building, visualizing, and managing digital twins, complete with built-in data connectors, simulation tools, and analytics dashboards.

Further Reading and Resources

For readers interested in going deeper—technically, strategically, or ethically—there's a growing body of literature and online communities worth exploring:

Books:

- Designing Digital Twins by Shyam Varan Nath – A practical, enterprise-oriented guide to planning and implementing digital twin solutions.
- Digital Twin Driven Smart Manufacturing by Fei Tao and Ang Liu – A deeper dive into digital twin use in manufacturing, with a focus on system architecture and industrial transformation.
- Human Compatible by Stuart Russell – While not about digital twins specifically, this book is critical for understanding the broader context of safe, aligned AI systems.

Organizations & Reports:
- Digital Twin Consortium – Offers industry case studies, open standards, and research on best practices across sectors.
- IEEE and ISO Standards Bodies – Publish emerging standards around digital twin architecture, security, and interoperability.
- McKinsey, Gartner, and Deloitte – Regularly release insight reports on trends in digital twin adoption, ROI, and future outlook.

Learning Platforms:
- Coursera, Udemy, and edX offer courses on digital twins, IoT, and simulation tools.
- GitHub repositories often include real-world projects, especially those using ROS, Unity, or USD.

- Medium, Towards Data Science, and NVIDIA's developer blog frequently feature real-world use cases and tutorials.

Whether you're a builder, a strategist, or a curious observer, the digital twin space is wide open and full of opportunity. These appendices are your map—but the journey is yours to define.

About the Author

Irvin K. Appell is a technology strategist, writer, and advocate for future-ready innovation. With a background spanning enterprise systems, AI integration, and digital transformation, he brings real-world insight to complex topics like digital twins, intelligent infrastructure, and the evolving relationship between humans and machines. His work sits at the intersection of business strategy and emerging tech—always grounded, always forward-thinking.

Irvin has advised companies across industries on how to turn data into decisions and systems into smarter, more adaptive environments. He believes technology should do more than optimize—it should empower. Digital Twin Technologies in Business is his first book, written to bridge the gap between technical depth and business relevance, and to help leaders make sense of where the future is headed—and how to get there responsibly.

When he's not writing or consulting, you'll find him exploring cities through the lens of urban systems, mentoring new tech talent, or staying curious about the next wave of change.

www.ingramcontent.com/pod-product-compliance
Lightning Source LLC
La Vergne TN
LVHW051429050326
832903LV00030BD/2985